Trish Morgan has packed so much into her life, and she shares with God has woven a rich tapestry w has been through. So buckle up and get ready for a great read.

Simon Guillebaud MBE
International Director of Great Lakes Outreach

'We simply said yes...' These four words found here in just one of many inspiring stories sum up for me the reason life is an unfolding adventure rather than a series of humdrum happenings for my friends Trish and Malc. Hang onto your hat as you join them on the journey she describes so well. I guarantee it will make you more ready than ever to 'simply say yes' to God too and see where he takes you!

Anthony Delaney
Senior Pastor, Ivy Church Manchester

Trish and Malcolm Morgan are the real deal. Their lives have inspired me for years. I have seen them consistently choose the narrow and costly way of following Jesus. That way has led them to consistent sacrificial generosity, while never giving up on the wild call of God that brings life. They are some of the few seasoned leaders who are still at the cutting edge of mission and have been from their twenties. Trish's writing has brought me to tears more than once in just a few pages. I hope this book gets read far and wide and inspires the next generation to live lives worth telling the story of. More is possible with Jesus and these pages sing that message of hope beautifully."

Miriam Swanson
Director of Fusion USA

An inspiring and hope-filled journey through a fascinating myriad of life experiences. Trish and Malc have left a strong legacy everywhere they have ministered - not least in Belfast, where they made an impact across the traditional divide. Honesty, integrity and humanity pour out of every page.

Chris Page
BBC Political Commentator
Northern Ireland

I've heard Trish share some of these stories in her testimony before, but as I now read them I'm saying out loud, "Wow! God you are amazing!" These stories are not here to impress you, they're here to inspire you and provoke you to imitation as you journey on your own adventure with Jesus.

John Harding
Senior Pastor, Frontline Church, Liverpool

Trish has a passion for God and for people that shines through every page of this book. You'll be inspired by the stories and experiences shared, but you'll also be energised to step out further into your own adventure of faith.

Cathy Madavan
Writer, Speaker and Author of 'Irrepressible'

I know you will be both inspired and challenged by this book, which is filled with God adventures. I have had the privilege of knowing Trish and Malc for many years and the phrase 'Yes Lord' steadied their steps through the many seasons they have faced on their journey of obedience.

Lynn Swart
Director, New Day United, South Africa

I am so proud of Trish and Malc whom I have known for many years since Heartbeat days. I believe the best is yet to come! Read this book and be inspired by the special and wonderful stories it contains and what God can do with a life that is totally surrendered to him.

Nancy Goudie

Author, Speaker, co-founder of NGM and founder of 'Spiritual Health Weekends'

HIGHER HEIGHTS, DEEPER SEAS

My Faith Adventures

Trish Morgan

First published in UK in 2022.

Copyright © Trish Morgan.

All rights reserved.

ISBN: 9798353855392

*Some names have had to be changed in the book to protect
identity.

Acknowledgements

So many people to thank so let's start with my wonderful family.

Malc, my partner in our crazy life adventures; Freya & Gavin, Aaron & Cat, Steve & Rachel, David and Dawn.

The trustees of Elpitha Hope UK who came on the incredible Greek chapter of my journey, Noel Gilmour, Andrew Brown, Greg Fane, Helen Pennington, Rachel Lindley and our amazing finance officer Gill Knott who has had tremendous patience with us as we navigated being charity directors. Their friendship, fellowship, prayer and financial support kept us going in days when we felt like giving up!

Frontline church Liverpool, who sent us with their blessing, journeyed with us through our highs and lows, triumphs and tragedies. Also Ivy church Manchester. We love you both and honour your missional hearts.

Thank you to all our financial supporters who gave when we shared a need for the work or anticipated personal cost.. I trust we were good stewards of what was given and can recount countless times where your giving made such a difference.

To those who agreed to read through this book or listen to my original ideas and then critiqued and corrected.

Thank you Sue Smith for initial feedback on my book. Thank you Joanna Hargreaves, Cathy Madavan, Nancy Goudie, Miriam Swanson, Liz Kaddour, Chris Page, Anthony Delaney, Simon Guillebaud and John Harding - a faithful, loving pastor to Malc and me. It's a blessing to know each of you and appreciate how you have helped me over the years.

My dear friends now around the world, Lizzie East, Mary Maguire, Rosey Shelbourne, Lynn Swart, Carol Dean, and a special shout out to the precious Greek friends who have enriched my life and extended my understanding of Greek life so much! Especially to Maria, whose story is shared in part here but whose journey in Jesus continues - you're a precious friend, keep going!

I'm so grateful for friends, laughter and love.
TM.

Dedications

In memory of my parents Derrick and Jean Maguire
who were wonderful examples in following and
serving Jesus.

My gorgeous grandchildren Reuben, Jesse, Talitha
and Jonah – Yia Yia loves you very much!

HIGHER HEIGHTS, DEEPER SEAS

Prelude		1
Intro:	MOVING TO GREECE	5
Verse 1:	AS FOR ME AND MY HOUSE	17
Verse 2:	HEARTBEAT: THE BAND YEARS	24
Verse 3:	LINCOLN, DAVID BECKHAM AND THE BBC	33
Chorus:	WHERE CAN I GO FROM YOUR SPIRIT?	43
Verse 4:	SOUTH AFRICA AND THE 94.7 BIKE RACE	44
Verse 5:	BELFAST DAYS	56
MID 8:	I BELIEVE IN MIRACLES	67
Bridge:	ROMANS 12: 1-2	72
Verse 6:	FRIENDSHIP, FAITH AND BIG PRAYERS	73
Chorus:	LOVED	83
Verse 7:	A SYRIAN LOVE STORY	84
Verse 8:	RITSONA REFUGEE CAMP	94
Verse 9:	DARK HOURS & TESTING TIMES	107
Outro :	UNFINISHED SYMPHONY	115

PRELUDE

Stevie Wonder had an album out when I was in my teens in 1976 called *Songs in the Key of Life*.

I played it endlessly. As a musician and songwriter, I have had the privilege to travel far and wide and combine my love of exploring new places, meeting new people and even getting to live in some amazingly beautiful countries. Threaded throughout it has been my Christian faith, which has led me on an incredible adventure of seeing God move and reveal His heart for this world and every human in it. I don't believe He has favourites, but I do think that faith that is living, active and obedient is a real blessing to His heart.

I would like to invite you on this journey.

We start in Greece where, until very recently, I was living. How did I get there and what happened along the way? If you are familiar with the Greek dancing song The Zorba or Sirtaki, as it's known in Greece, you'll know it begins rather sedately and slowly, but by the time you have danced yourself round and round in a circle, with your arms placed on your fellow dancers' shoulders you are increasingly aware the pace has picked up somewhat and the ending can sometimes seem rather crazy and disorientating. The last nine years have occasionally felt like that, especially with Covid 19 turning everything upside down, and inside out. Moreover, we are still navigating our way out.

There's the introduction! Then we will start at the beginning. If this book is to resemble the way a song is constructed, then the verses will be chapters of my life from early times with my parents and their influence on me and the discovery of music, which has been a passion all my days. I've been married 38 years, having met Malcolm, my husband, in my early twenties. When we married, we immediately started travelling with a band playing Contemporary Christian music. The band was called Heartbeat and I will cover the story of our time together and the song that went into the UK singles charts in 1987.

Four years into our marriage, I had twins, Freya and Aaron. As a family of four, we moved to new cities, mainly throughout the UK until 2004 when we began to move overseas. We have lived in South Africa, Northern Ireland, and Greece, and had incredible experiences in each country.

I think I missed my real calling of starting a removals business; we've certainly spent a lot of time packing and relocating. However, I have loved looking back as I've remembered people, places, emotions and the deep friendships we now have with folks from many nations and cultures.

Some friends we may never see again. Some of the stories I tell of how we stumbled into our refugee work in Greece could be told to music played in a minor key. We saw unbelievable suffering, neglect, and trauma, but also bravery, tenacity and the kindness of strangers that counterbalances the tragedy. In at least one of those stories you could play a full-on love song at top volume. It was during our time in Greece we founded a charity based in England called Elpitha Hope UK.

Sometimes when you write a song you put in a middle section of music - often eight bars that we call a mid eight. It creates an additional flavour to the song and can modulate up or down a key and change in rhythm too amongst other options.

I believe in miracles is my Mid 8. I also recount stories like the times I met influential politicians, for instance meeting Martin McGuinness just before THAT HANDSHAKE with Her Majesty the Queen in 2011.

Spending a day with David Beckham filming with the BBC for a show called Live and Kicking which featured my two kids is up there as an amazing story too.

But so are the ordinary people I've met who were suddenly caught up in extraordinary circumstances, or who had incredible encounters with a God who listens to our cries, hears, and cares.

The chorus or hook, as it used to be known, will I hope keep pulsating throughout. The theme of the chorus would be that life is unpredictable and my choice was to live outside of my comfort zones.

But there, out on some crazy edge, I found that my relationship with God grew. He matches my steps and goes beyond, then invites me to go higher and deeper with Him in my faith journey.

May you be inspired, laugh, shed a tear or two, or learn to take risks; for this is what life looks like to me. Music moves us, and when you can get to know the greatest composer of all time, it all makes sense.

I hope this book will be like a song you will keep in your head and heart for years to come, long after the person who wrote it has left the stage and the final note has finished resounding. Cue the song

MOVING TO GREECE

Climbing up a slippery granite walkway to the fort's lookout posts I took one last deep breath and stood still in wonder. Feeling my lungs going back to a normal rhythm and my heart slowing down, I looked at the amazing sight of the city and surrounding areas of Chalkida, in Greece. It was 2013 and we were becoming increasingly drawn to this city, to the point we were considering living and working there.

Beside me was my husband Malc, and the only friend we had in the city, Eleni, as we surveyed the different views in front of us.

Firstly, the stunningly beautiful azure blue waters of the Evripos strait flowing straight out into the Aegean Sea with a few large ships anchored, waiting to come into port.

Our eyes focussed on the suspension bridge linking the mainland to the island of Evia, with cars and lorries crossing to and fro and the overloaded vans spluttering out their fumes. I wondered how such battered vehicles passed their MOT.

Serving as a ghostly backdrop, on the outskirts of Chalkida we saw the closed cement factory that once employed 5,000 people. When it closed many men in their 50s and 60s had become long-term unemployed. It looked desolate.

Following the train railway line, which hugs the coast, brings you to the other side of Chalkida, which strangely is on the mainland again. There is another ancient bridgehead, now modernised to open and shut each night.

Ships of all shapes and sizes parade through the Evripos, navigating the fiercely rapid tide 'Trella Nera.' or 'Crazy Waters', with their crews waving to onlookers during this nightly ritual.

The city itself is hemmed in by hills.

As far as planning has allowed (if that exists in Greece) the apartment blocks, houses, churches, banks, schools, clinics, and thousands of little shops seem to be squeezed into a very small area; the waterfront is bustling with the hotels, bars, cafes and restaurants that are essential for the Greeks to make a living.

And here we were, standing, surveying and praying, 'Lord... what is it you want us to do here?' At this point in 2013, the country was in a deep recession, which would become even more severe, and to our knowledge only a couple of 'Protestant' churches existed, with mainly elderly congregations of possibly 100 combined. Greater Chalkida has a population of 120,000 people.

We began to pray for households of faith in each district and pictured lights burning for Jesus in the neighbourhoods. We knew instantly this would be our vision for Chalkida and the surrounding districts for the next few years. We would live in this city, pray for this city, ask for people of peace, love the person in front of us and just trust Him to create more of these households of faith in time.

Where to live was our first question. We felt somewhere central to the city was important and a few months before had been prophesied a room with a view!

We had left a lovely rented townhouse in the hills of Belfast, Northern Ireland which overlooked the city and lough, but the day had come to pack up and leave. Our time of overseeing City Church Belfast was coming to an end and I found myself packing and moving house for what felt like the umpteenth time in my life.

Feeling rather weary of this process and a little sorry for myself, I was having a chat/mini-moan to The Lord. 'OK, Lord... I'm following your plan but sometimes this packing lark is tiring and costly.' I threw open the double doors of my kitchen that gave me the city view and pondered it for a few moments. Then I simply said 'Wherever you take us next, please can I have a view like this? Amen'

I barely even remembered the whispered prayer, but a few days later I had an amazing moment.

It was our final few weeks in Belfast and we were sitting in Starbucks with a wonderful friend called Lynn Swart. We had met many years previously through a national worship leaders' forum I had attended. It wasn't hard to meet Lynn; apart from one other woman, it was us two amid the many other guys! She was South African but living in the UK and because of my previous introduction to South Africa through my Heartbeat band days we hit it off straight away. Over the years we kept in touch and eventually Lynn became instrumental in my visiting South Africa in the late 1990s, not long after Nelson Mandela had become a free man and then President of the nation.

Somehow, every time we were at significant times of transition, Lynn would be around to encourage us, cheer us on, and bless us with her ministry in our church. She had been our guest speaker before we handed over, and was leading a dynamic community church in South Belfast, Northern Ireland when we were released into this new, unknown journey.

It just so happened a good friend of hers and a prophet was also ministering in the city. She asked to meet up with him, so while they caught up at one end of a table we were having a lovely time with the young guy who had travelled with this prophet.

At the end, with minimal information, Lynn invited this guy to pray for us. We had met him before but didn't know him that well. He prayed very sincerely: a prayer that unfortunately I can't remember now. As we thanked him, he turned to go, but then stopped. Looking straight at me he said 'Trish, by the way, the Lord says he's going to give you a room with a view in your next house'. WOW. I stood stunned at this pinpoint word of encouragement. I had barely made it a prayer, and now here it was coming right back at me, through someone who barely knew me. These kind of moments don't happen every day and it was so reassuring that God had this whole move in His hands. I was only regretting that I hadn't asked for a million pounds!

We left Belfast in January 2013; heavy snow had fallen and the hill we lived at the top of was looking extremely pretty, albeit a challenge for drivers. I was struggling with tonsillitis, so was already feeling rough. And emotionally it wasn't easy to pack up and leave.

We took the ferry across to Scotland then travelled down into England where we sojourned with our friends who led an amazing urban church in Liverpool called Frontline. We had had connections with them for the past seven years, and it felt right to harbour with them while praying through this crazy idea of moving to Greece without a job, house or salary... or not!

Let me just pause to mention that knowing what God is saying and being obedient is really important. Many people struggle with hearing God, and, while I'm no expert, there are a few guidelines we go by when we know a major shift in our lives is coming. We often begin with a thought that comes in quiet times, when we are reading the bible, or praying. When God told us to start praying for Greece in the beginning of 2012, it was literally like that. I wrote it down. Fairly soon after I felt I needed to vocalise the thought and shared it with Malc. It is always good to bring your partner or a trusted friend in on the journey as soon as you can.

Then, over a period of time, through listening, sharing with respected peers, leadership in your home church, and friends, you maybe decide to visit the place you sense God may be leading you. With Greece, we had three visits.

In those visits we looked, listened, met others, asked questions, some very practical, and then the pace began to gather. Maybe prophetic words come, maybe a friend contacts you to share a scripture or thought they had while praying. As you begin to document all this, you go by the peace in your heart.

Within our marriage, we both need to agree on any major decision, it's no good one of us trying to force a decision on the other. Sadly, we've seen that happen too many times where one of the partners in the relationship can end up resenting a move or disruption and hardship that comes from such adventures in faith.

To be honest, the next nine months were a real mixed bag of celebrations, joy, frustration and difficulty.

One moment of joy was our son Aaron marrying his long-term girlfriend Catherine. They had met at university in Reading and had been dating for over five years. We also returned to South Africa for a month to visit our friends at The Barn Church Johannesburg where we had lived and ministered, and we visited Cape Town too. We have so many happy memories of our time in South Africa.

While out there a couple we had got to know pledged some financial support to us It gave us the first boost to thinking Greece could work – the first building block.

Back in the UK, I took a part-time media job at Frontline Church, which was incredibly helpful. Our house was in storage and we still had on-going costs of over £700 each month without renting or paying other bills.

Then there were the difficulties. Malc couldn't do temporary teaching as we had hoped, as new government rules required him to give weeks of his time for free before he could return to a classroom. We simply couldn't afford for him not to earn so he decided to take a 'Teaching English as a Foreign Language' course, which, once completed, opened up local language schools for him. There wasn't much work and he had to sign on unemployed for a few weeks, which felt strange considering we were processing a call to mission, but we simply needed the finance and tried not to overthink the reasons why we were in this position.

Malc wasn't able to teach for long as he was asked to visit his brother who was dying of cancer in Spain.

The trip abroad disrupted his unemployment benefits, but Malc went out to be with his brother in his final days and spent many hours by his bedside as he slowly slipped away aged 59. We were in Greece on our final recce when he died and sadly the week we thought we had there ended up being only three days

11

for Malc. I stayed in Greece with Eleni while Malc flew to Spain to deal with his brother's funeral. Unfortunately, due to the recession there were no direct routes, so he had to fly via Zurich. It took two days to fly there. Our travel insurance didn't cover this cost – they would only return him to the UK in such circumstances.

Before he left, Eleni had mentioned there was a language school in Chalkida looking for English-speaking teachers. Malc phoned and was asked to go immediately for an interview. He walked into the interview in his shorts and flip-flops. He was offered a part-time post there and then, starting in September. Here was another building block.

Feeling this was the confirmation we needed, he left for Spain leaving me to start looking at the city of Chalkida as our next move. I hired a car for a few days and proceeded to merrily go round in circles; Chalkida had a deeply confusing one-way system. However, I did manage to stop at streets/areas I felt looked nice to live in and took a few photos.

Fast forward to early September 2013; Malc went ahead of me to Greece to start his part-time teaching job, I was finishing up a few weeks later working on some media projects for the church in Liverpool. By now our fantastic kids had left home and were settled in jobs in Reading and York. This time they weren't coming with us, which made it doubly hard not having company for us but easier when it came to the space required!

We had hoped to have at least one other couple come out with us but after several conversations with interested parties something cropped up in each case where they felt it wasn't the right time to join us. We were left to pioneer this move on our own. It makes such a difference when there is no community already in place to help you settle in and truthfully it wasn't easy. Malc was tasked with finding somewhere for us to live and was led on wild goose chases for a few weeks. The economy had crashed so there weren't any real estate shops anymore and all the websites seemed out of date by a few years.

But we found one website which had what we thought was a great sounding apartment at an affordable rent, Malc called the guy, who met him outside an empty shop.

Quickly he realised this apartment was 11 kilometres away. That was not what we wanted. 'Hmmm, OK' said the agent, 'there is a place I know very close to here and by the sea. It's one of the most modern buildings and may be too expensive but let me show you.'

Malc called me. He had seen a place that was spacious and modern but was sounding hesitant and I asked what the problem was. 'Well,' he said 'It's completely empty: no oven, no light fittings, no curtains... nothing'. This is apparently common in Greece; they literally take all furnishings including lighting fittings, ovens, and air conditioners too!

'That's OK,' I said. 'We can ship our furniture out. Is it by the sea?' He said it was, then showed me pictures with the most panoramic view of the other side of the bay and a beautiful view of the sea stretching for miles.

It was a WOW moment. I couldn't believe Malc was so hesitant until I realised this view came with a price tag. After some discussions I said 'This looks like our home. Offer the owner €150 less, and if he accepts... it's ours.'

The owners did kindly accept our offer. They probably preferred having UK pounds come in than local renters who seemingly were not very reliable. We moved in with very little furniture, although Eleni helped us with some garden furniture we used indoors and we bought a few things from IKEA. Second-hand shops for furniture were and still are non-existent in Greece. Everything seems to be kept in the family and passed around or handed down.

For the next three months we faced the toughest, most stripped-back life we'd probably ever experienced since we had married 30 years earlier, not just materially but socially as well.

For Malc it wasn't as bad. He went to teach most days but for me, I knew only Eleni in the entire city and she was a busy lawyer working mainly in Athens – 80 kilometres away. For a person whose strength finder is 'connectedness' it was isolation of the highest degree. Even with beautiful views and walks around the sea and city I felt very lonely in a strange place, not speaking the language well and getting to grips with the Greek way of life which enthralled me and frustrated me in equal measures.

But I had my view. Each day I would get up, walk to the lounge, open up the shutters and just gaze at what seemed like a different palette of colour. I'd make a coffee and sit in silence listening to the fishermen talk out on their boats in the water, the birds singing and the gulls following the fishing trawlers. From this balcony we once watched a bluefin tuna swim into the bay; it resembled a dolphin but without quite the same grace or tail. We also watched seals, and each spring we would watch the UK Red Arrows display team scream across the skies practising their forthcoming air display routines with the coloured smoke left to evaporate into the clear blue skies.

We had a few friends come out from Liverpool and Belfast eight weeks after moving out. What a lifeline they were for us. They came and encouraged, worshipped, prayed, laughed, ate with us and gave us courage to face our task of pioneering a community of faith over the coming months.

In January 2014 our contents arrived from the UK. As we unpacked, I pulled out my old Sony Vaio laptop. Turning it on after many months I checked through the documents and photos I might have missed swapping across to my new Samsung tablet. On the laptop were photos from my random hire car drive around Chalkida nine months earlier, while looking for a home. To my shock and amazement I had stopped outside the very road we now lived in and had taken photos of our specific apartment block. Who knew?

AS FOR ME AND MY HOUSE

There's a story in the Old Testament where the people of Israel had escaped captivity from the Egyptians and were resettling into their newly found land. Their leader Joshua gave them a challenge. 'Choose this day who are you going to serve.' It's a great question. Throughout history we have always had a choice. We haven't been programmed to be robotic in our thinking or actions. In fact, the human being is fearfully and wonderfully made! Creative, intuitive, intelligent, resourceful, humorous... I could go on but you get my drift. As we grow up we are influenced by many things. Personally, I was raised in a house of faith. It seemed normal to me to share my meal table with people who were not from my family. Sometimes we would even have visitors at breakfast time. My parents were always busy with paid jobs as teacher and health visitor, raising four kids and also growing a faith community from our home. My father had actually been a Baptist Minister, having trained at Trinity College, Dublin and he met my mum while she was a midwife in Exeter, in North Devon. My mum hadn't come from a faith household at all; in fact it was quite the opposite – her father had banned her from church as he was an agnostic.

My dad had been brought up with a Northern Irish faith in a Protestant culture and was clearly defined in his views. When my older brother married a Catholic girl many years later, it caused a huge family row on my dad's side of the family. But my parents always strove to be open to other expressions of the Christian faith and we always had the choice as to which denomination we felt drawn towards.

I found an understanding of God loving me and his invitation to follow him at a young age. I wrestled with my faith as a teenager but was also part of an extraordinary move of God in my town and school. I loved the excitement of our meetings and the exuberant worship and fun we had in our youth. I joined a travelling choir singing a musical written by Jamie and Carol Owens called Come Together. It was exciting to be able to meet other teens who had a faith in Jesus too.

I loved music. Music became and remains my number one expression in my life. I was taught piano for a few years but struggled with connecting the music I could read to the playing of it. I was so slow, but I could play by ear and I found that was quicker and more fun, and I loved improvisation. I would watch other musicians play, ask them to teach me the chords I could hear, augmented 7ths and so on, and soon I became our community church's lead musician with a bunch of other budding musicians. I learnt by listening to records and playing along. I loved all forms of music, especially soul music. However, my parents and I clashed a lot about this, and I ended up smuggling contemporary pop music into our home in the sleeves of a

Christian album. I would be listening to Andrae Crouch one minute and Stevie Wonder the next!

After a few years of playing and singing I began writing songs, some of which other people wanted to use and sing. It was my dream to be in music full-time but I also needed a paying career and I felt equally attracted to nursing. In 1977 I went off to The Royal London Hospital in Whitechapel to train as a nurse.

I loved my nursing years. I learnt a lot, saw incredible operations, held dying patients' hands, watched ICU patients recover and leave completely better, and found camaraderie in my group of friends. Some great friendships started as we shared accommodation; to this day many of us have kept in contact and remained good friends. It just so happened that at this point I joined the Christian Union, which was open to all medical disciplines. We had dentists, medics, nurses, and physiotherapists in our midst. Before we knew it, we were growing exponentially in numbers, with more and more people committing to following Jesus.

I was put in charge of the CU worship team and things really started to take off. Looking back, some might have called it revival; we had an incredible group of friends who passionately loved Jesus and yet were ready to have a laugh too. These many friends are now your GPs, church leaders, Overseas Aid workers. Many of them are soon to be retired, no doubt!

I passed my Registered General Nurse exams and worked as a staff nurse for a year then, through a mixture of a broken heart from a relationship that didn't last, and God clearly speaking to me, I took a six-month gap, travelling to New Zealand to live with a family who were friends of my parents from the established faith community in my home town in the UK.

Strangely enough, within a few weeks the church they attended in Auckland decided to have a camp with another church and in this incredible 'historic' camp they decided to merge. In the process, I found myself directly in contact with their worship team leaders Dave and Dale Garratt who were pioneers of the modern Christian worship movement that was being created, and an excellent songwriter called Brent Chambers. These guys were forerunners of new church music called 'Scripture in Song' with contemporary Holy-Spirit-filled songs that I had been singing in the UK. I now found myself sitting at their feet!

While in Auckland, I found a band willing to incorporate me and we did some concerts, got interviewed on radio stations. I felt excited and convinced that this was what I wanted to do as a career. Towards the end of my six months there, I was asked if I would consider staying on to work with the Garratts. However, although I thought it was an awesome opportunity, I felt I needed to return to the UK.

Just before my big trip abroad I had begun a friendship with a guy from my brother's university days. He was easy-going, fun, a faith guy and very handsome. Now a PE teacher, he was keeping in touch with me via the old blue airmail letters and the odd long distance phone call; it felt to me like he could be my life partner. His name was Malcolm; after a few letters I had written, he asked me politely to spell his name right! Malc was a brilliant youth worker; he was heading up the youth in his church in Rochford. When I returned from New Zealand via Australia we began to pursue our relationship more seriously.

On my return journey to the UK I had an amazing moment of faith. The ticket I had bought to go round the world was with a cheap airline called Laker Airways. Unfortunately, they went into liquidation while I was in Australia. In those days there were no obligations to fly stranded people back to their destination and, by the time I arrived at Sydney airport the airline had been out of business for three weeks!

I managed the first leg of my flight to LA with the airline Qantas who honoured my ticket. However, the next part from the US to the UK was causing problems as no-one was accepting my ticket.

I decided to turn up to the airport anyway, hand in my ticket to a British Airways desk and ask very nicely if they could help me out. For some reason or other they couldn't do anything for me straightaway and I was asked to come back the next day. I befriended a girl at the airport who was distraught. She was also stranded with a Laker ticket and in tears. We hung out together, stopped over in a cheap hostel overnight and went back the next day. I really didn't have much money and not even a credit card, so being held up in the USA for days on end not knowing anyone wasn't looking like a good idea to me. I returned to the same desk as the day before. By now the girl with me was in an emotional meltdown at the possibility of being stuck in America. I decided to pray in front of her, thanking God for our seats on the plane and asking Him to take care of us.

I handed over my Invalid ticket. The lady smiled and asked me to wait at the side with my friend. We stood and watched all these people file past us onto the plane and then heard the gate announcement that it was closing shortly.

Once everyone had gone through, she called me forward, handed me a ticket and with a smile wished me a safe journey home. She did the same to my friend. I thanked her endlessly and passed through the gate. As we boarded the plane it became clear she had accidentally doubled up on the seats, as someone was sitting in my allocated chair. I waited for a stewardess to help us. She looked at me and said 'OK miss, follow me please.' We headed towards the front of the plane and for a split second I thought they were taking us off, but she stopped at some very spacious seats, waved me in and said, 'With the compliments of British Airways'! I was now in business class. 'Flip me!' said my new friend. 'That's a brilliant answer to your prayer – thanks God!' she said, laughing through her tears. I sank into my seat, feeling deeply relieved. I just wanted the door to shut so I could know I was going home in style to my family. When I returned, Malc and I began our relationship very consciously. He moved nearer to where I lived and took substitute teaching jobs.

Meanwhile I found myself unemployed for the first nine months back in the UK. I wondered if I had made the right decision turning down the Garratts, but I wanted to do what they were doing in New Zealand in the UK.

I took agency nursing when I could but the country was in the middle of a recession and few nursing jobs were available. Eventually, I got a temporary job in a local private hospital. On the first night shift I turned up just as the staff were being told they were closing the whole building and everyone was losing their jobs. For a moment I felt like Jonah. Maybe I wasn't trusting God when He had said he would use me in music and here I was, still trying to work in nursing. Was I really trusting Him to lead me? Even in my early twenties I was learning invaluable lessons of faith, not looking to the material circumstances but leaning into a riskier but faith-filled life of adventure with God. Malc and I embraced that future together and, after a few years of dating, we married and became involved in a full-time ministry team and music band called Heartbeat.

HEARTBEAT: THE BAND YEARS

'COME ON AND CELEBRATE'

Come on and celebrate,
His gift of love we will celebrate,
The Son of God who loved us
And gave us life.

We'll shout your praise O king,
You give us joy nothing else can bring,
We'll give to you our offering,
In celebration praise.

Chorus.
Come on and Celebrate, Celebrate, Celebrate and sing
Celebrate and sing to The King,
Come in and Celebrate, Celebrate, Celebrate and sing,
Celebrate and sing to the king.

P. Morgan & D. Bankhead
©Thank-you Music 1984

In 1982 I had an opportunity that I had desired since I was a teenager – to sing full-time in a band.

Through earlier connections when I had performed at some music events in London, I had kept in touch with a couple called Ray and Nancy Goudie. They were the full-time leaders of a music band for Youth for Christ and they toured the UK supporting church outreach and school events for young people.

Out of the blue I took a phone call back in my parent's house in Bradford-on-Avon after my New Zealand adventure; it was Ray. He explained the previous singer had left quite quickly so they needed a replacement immediately to fulfil some bookings. Was I free for the coming weekend? There was a special tour on; they were due to play a couple of songs each night and needed a lead singer.

I said yes! A mixture of excitement and then worry hit me all at once. What if I couldn't learn the songs in time, or I got a cold and lost my voice?

I took a train to the Midlands on the Friday and a man who was a good friend of Ray and Nancy picked me up in his Range Rover.

As I sat in the back being driven to North Wales, I was literally handed a cassette player, tape and headphones, and in the back of a car I was learning three new songs to sing that night with a band I had never met. It was a baptism of fire. I had worked with bands before but each has its own style and chemistry. They were polite to me but I could sense some wariness as to who I was and what I would bring to the team. On the road with us on those few nights was a well-known drama group who were excellent. I enjoyed meeting them too.

On the final night the lead actor decided to let me know that I didn't fit the image of the band. He criticised my outfits and my stage presence, and left me bruised by his opinions. I hadn't invited his comments; he just gave them.

Despite that unsavoury moment once the tour had finished, I was contacted not long after and was invited to join the band. I was relieved, as I had worried that this man's opinion might have coloured Ray's judgement of me. Obviously, God had the final say. When I said yes, it began a journey of musical discovery and one of faith that was foundational for the way we live today.

I began writing many songs and loved performing them and getting to record in a studio and release singles and LPs. Towards the end of my time with Heartbeat, we were making CDs. Probably one of the most popular songs I wrote was 'Come on and Celebrate'. I loved playing a real piano and my parents had one in their living room. I was staying with them before I married and would often sit at the piano playing songs and writing. As we were often hosting celebration events where churches would meet together, I wanted to write a song that used that word: 'Celebrate'. To my knowledge it hadn't been used before in a worship context so I started with 'Come on and Celebrate'. While

I was away on honeymoon the lads of the band got together and worked on the song; when I returned, they played me their lines. I liked it and the finished song quickly became a regular in our play list. Being in a band and working with other songwriters I learnt how to write better, be critical in my skill and level-headed about my ability. It wasn't always easy and it certainly kept you humble.

In 1983 the National Youth for Christ organisation had a change of leadership and direction. It was at this point as a band that we decided to stay together and become a full-time faith ministry and relocate to Malmesbury, Wiltshire, becoming a community of musicians and friends who enjoyed being together, sharing our homes and possessions and living a life of mission. We had no blueprint to follow but were going on this crazy faith journey and loving the God-inspired moments along the way.

We had been based around Birmingham and Wolverhampton before that; to rehearse we needed to be staying with other people and on the road you stayed with hundreds of different hosts. I had rarely slept in my own bed for those two years. The move to Malmesbury changed that. Over a few years our band expanded not just with musicians but tech staff, administrators, and Malc, who joined as a youth worker and 'MC' for concerts. It became a worshipping and evangelistic community.

We toured the UK a lot, often travelling home in the early hours of the morning. We saw God do some incredible healings as we played our songs at concerts and began to realise that the Holy

Spirit was working in our concerts, at times so powerfully that unexplained things happened that to this day make us smile. People who had no faith would tell us that, during a song, intense heat would be evident in their bodies and they would be healed of bad backs, damaged ligaments, broken bones and so on. They would talk to us afterwards, asking us 'What is this and was this really God at work?' We began writing more and more worship songs that we could use in our sets mixed in with other performance material. It was often in the worship songs that the atmosphere in the room changed, mostly for good. However, occasionally it felt like we were getting opposition and resistance.

At one point we released a single, which made it into the charts. It was called 'Tears from Heaven'. It was a collaborative track with five others writing it together. It went into the main UK singles chart at no 32. The night we heard it might have made the top 40, we were nervously listening to the Sunday evening radio top 40 show and had to wait like everyone else to hear if our single had charted. As we sat around a small radio in fellow band members Ian and Dorry's house the presenter announced a new entry, the minute we heard our name we went crazy. Unfortunately, Ian and Dorry's little baby cried as we were making too much noise! We toured and travelled so much and it was great to know that many fans were buying the single.

It went as high as no 21 in the commercial radio charts. We were beside Diana Ross' song 'Chain Reaction' and other well-known 1987 bands. I was heavily pregnant with twins and was actually in hospital when the band went to sing on Top of the Pops, but it was still fun being part of it all and the buzz it generated at the time. When the band visited me in hospital it was really funny to see the nursing staff's faces as they realised the local West Country band were both in the charts and on their ward!

As folk married and set up home we shared our houses and learnt many things about sharing everything you had with others. For the first 18 months, Malc and I lived with the founders of the ministry, Ray and Nancy Goudie and loved them very much. They were good fun and also good role models for us to pursue Jesus in every way we possibly could.

We gave sacrificially to each other and the ministry, believing we needed to seed into the ministry ourselves before asking outsiders for donations. As we became successful in our music and released albums, we returned the profits into the ministry occasionally getting a share out at the end of each month once all Heartbeat bills had been paid. When it came to provision we saw amazing answers to prayer. When Malc and I married we talked about the promise from 1 Kings Chapter 17 which is about the widow whose pot of oil never ran out. We had both come from professions where, if we had stayed in them, we would have had a good house, pension and a comfortable lifestyle. We asked God to keep us in a standard of living which would be sufficient for us, as we wanted children and extra to bless others with. After 38 years of living either with a salary or not, I can say God has been faithful. We have known hard times financially which at times has been painful but we have also known abundance and it's been an incredible journey, which isn't finished yet.

In 1990, Malc and I felt our time in the band and team ministry had come to an end. We wanted to pursue a different challenge and left to live in Belfast Northern Ireland, joining a highly creative church in the city centre. Malc picked up full-time paid employment with the YMCA.

It was as if, once we had made our decision to live in a city, join a local church, and get involved with whatever God was doing, we always found more doors and opportunities came our way.

As the years went by, I was invited to lead worship at National events and leadership conferences. I became more involved in leading worship wherever I lived, either in local church or at big national events. I loved singing and playing the keyboard and hearing voices singing God's praise together.

As they grew up, my kids watched and learned that who you are at home as a parent is who you are on stage: platform should make no difference to your heart of worship, whether you are dealing with one person or 1,000 people. They became musicians in their own right and, in their teens, I began to take them out to events to sing and play in my teams.

In my early years of leading worship, I encountered a ceiling of men only leading in ministry. It was difficult at times to navigate this, as I had never thought of gifting being allotted to a specific gender, I was just happy to be involved in music and worship and didn't want to have to deal with the big theological reasons as to why I should or shouldn't be leading. At times it was awkward, and looking back in that male dominated environment it was hard to be taken seriously. I think women had to work really hard at being given opportunities that men took for granted. At one event I took a male worship leader with me. It was my invite and band but I wanted to give him more platform and experience, so we did a major bible week together. One night the worship just took off; it was electrifying. Afterward, this guy jumped onto the stage and proceeded to thank me, compliment the way I had led. It was a welcome gesture and I thanked him for his kind words. Then, after walking past me he approached my male counterpart, took out his diary and proceeded to ask this guy to come and take a worship event back at his home church and maybe arrange a few more gigs to boot! Often, while socialising either before or after an event, I would be asked by local organisers if I had children and who was looking after them while I was away. I never heard them ask the guys in the band that question.

Thankfully my daughter has not had to endure half as much difficulty when it comes this area of discrimination but we still have a way to go in re-dressing the gender imbalance. I've been so grateful to Malc who has often had to remind the male leaders we have worked with that they have a responsibility to think about and make room for women in ministry and leadership. He doesn't do this in a condescending way but with a conviction that we are better together than competing!

LINCOLN, DAVID BECKHAM AND THE BBC

In 1993, we moved to Lincoln, England from Belfast. Malc took a teaching post in a unit for pupils who had been removed from mainstream schooling. My work had me travelling with bands or working on local radio and TV stations.

Besides a busy family life we decided to do foster training. We had always wanted to have more children, but I was poorly after the twins were born so we decided to explore fostering or adoption, if the opportunity arose. One lady in our church in Lincoln was a social worker; she enrolled us onto the fostering and adoption course. What an eye-opener. It took six months from training to screening before we began to accept little ones mainly aged one to five years old, just for respite care. My travelling made a long term placement too onerous on the family. More often than not, the phone call would come on a Friday afternoon near 5pm and within 30 minutes the young child would arrive with a social worker, often with its possessions in a black plastic bag. We wouldn't know the little one's routine or any preferences, but knew accepting them helped the parent get a breather or respite, while they were in hospital, for example. We all muddled on with my kids loving having a younger child in the home and realising not every family has a stable environment to grow up in. Some kids were OK. Often their single mum was not coping.

So many people, especially Christians, have opinions on abortion, but not as many are at the other end when a baby is born into a disadvantaged home where there are all sorts of reasons why having a child becomes a struggle, not a joy.

I do believe in the sanctity of life from conception but felt challenged to do more than have an opinion.

It was strangely at this point in time that several leaders in our church got concerned we were taking on too much. They were right: we were overseeing the youth work as well as young adults; I was on the worship leadership team, co-leading a monthly district congregation of 200 + and Malc was involved in a wider apostolic network called Groundlevel.

So we decided to drop one of our leadership roles in the church to make room for fostering, probably not the answer the church leaders had been hoping for but we felt peace about the decision.

One night, as Malc and I were going out to a meeting, one of our twins said in a plaintive voice... 'You're not going out again are you?' I glanced at Malc. I said to him, 'Did you HEAR that?' We did, and in that moment we knew we would have to take another look at our time commitments, especially for Malc to re-consider his full-time work. We needed to release this immense time pressure we were both feeling. We were simply out too much, and our kids were fed up.

Later that school year, we had an amazing opportunity to move short-term out to Johannesburg in South Africa, from January to July.

We had responded to an invitation from a church whose leaders we had met on previous visits and we really felt called to explore our links with them. Our kids were in the top class in primary school at that point; they were already earmarked to go to a local senior school nearby which was extremely popular. After discussing it thoroughly with friends we decided to take this six-month opportunity as a natural time where the kids schooling wasn't going to be too disrupted. We were effectively taking a gap year with no salary coming in and no promises from the church that had invited us to pay us. As it transpired, we never were paid. I had a few thousand pounds coming in each year from musical royalties and there were a few folk who wanted to support us in this season of mission we were embarking on.

Malc and I have taken risks, but not over-extended crazy ones (or so we think). We always felt that we wanted to live life as a God-inspired adventure for ourselves and our children and we were given unique opportunities that others didn't have. It sometimes meant leaving the security of job and home – something that many people simply cannot do. We like singing about risk-taking on Sundays but the comfort zone is the place where the majority of people inside and outside of the church live.

The six months went fast, we sampled South African life, helped develop certain areas of the church life, visited townships and loved it but felt our connection to the main leaders wasn't going to work in the long term so happily returned to Lincoln to live the next five years in our own home.

We had rented out our house in Lincoln at this time but had taken a small container of home comforts to South Africa. We had initially hoped the inviting church could have accommodated us, but a few weeks before we were due to arrive there had been a massive upset in the church with some staff being 'retrenched' (made redundant). The accommodation situation was one of the on-going sensitive issues. So, our home in the UK was once again a little sparse until our stuff arrived back.

September came and it was time for the twins to start in their new school.

Malc worked his notice for a term as we began to transition him into working full-time for New Life Church in Lincoln.

A few weeks into the new term I was home when I took a phone call out of the blue.

'Is that Mrs Morgan? Do you have twin children called Aaron and Freya?' I was taken a little aback by the caller knowing this much already, but I confirmed it was me, and then was told that the phone call was coming from the production office of a BBC children's programme called Live and Kicking.

'We have just read a wonderful letter from your daughter Freya. She has written to us as we have a competition about making people's dreams come true, to ask if we can make her twin brother's dream come true by watching Manchester United play'.

The phone call went on to explain how they were in the early stages of trying to see if this could happen. But they asked whether, if it was possible, Aaron could go up to Manchester with us as a family, as it might be on a school day. For now, she left me getting excited about this possibility for Aaron. It was true he does support Manchester United – how and why I'm not sure about as both Malc and myself are avid Liverpool supporters but hey, we're all up for kids following their own choices!

I think it was the very next day the researcher called back, this time rather excited that not only could they offer this but that David Beckham was available and had agreed to take a training session for Aaron's football team! So now not only had we to keep it a secret till the following Saturday when Aaron would get the surprise phone call from the programme live on television but I had to go and ask the school if it would be possible for this new team, who had only been playing a few weeks, to have a day off, travel to Manchester and meet David Beckham while being filmed by the BBC!

I went up to the school and nervously asked the receptionist if there was any way I could speak to the head of PE about something rather confidential. No matter which way you look at this I instantly must have come across as a fussy, over-protective mum. 'What exactly is it concerning?' asked the receptionist to which I replied I was unable to let her know but please could she let me speak to the PE teacher and it would become clear. She phoned him and, true to form, he said he was busy... I said it was very important and I would wait. A little while later she invited me into a reception room. I asked if it would be possible for only her and the teacher to hear the conversation. I can only imagine this receptionist thinking 'we've got a right one here'. And believe me, I was beginning to feel rather weird about it all myself. However, fortunately she agreed. I told the teacher whose parent I was.

He thought for one moment I was trying to get Aaron into the first-year team squad. Aaron had only played one game so far, I think. But I had to come clean. As I told him the situation with the BBC he began to laugh with disbelief. The receptionist was shaking and couldn't believe her ears. I assured him I wasn't making it up and that if he called the BBC they would confirm. Thank God he believed me.

Unsurprisingly the PE staff and an entire first year squad including Freya were given permission for a day off, and, after the exciting phone call from Live and Kicking on the Saturday morning Aaron was now in on the secret! Bless him, he was overwhelmed when he took the phone call and could hardly believe it was happening.

It was early October and we all piled onto the bus to head to Altrincham where the TV recording was to take place.

We arrived to find a TV crew, presenters, directors, cameramen and a coaching team on behalf of Adidas (David Beckham's sponsors), all to meet us little lot from Lincoln!

Freya was going to be filming with David Beckham about her letter and then he was going to take the team through a few training tips for the cameras. For some reason, Malcolm and I hadn't brought anything with us for filming. I probably thought it wouldn't be allowed but the head of PE at the school was out with his camcorder. However, to this day I have never seen the footage!

About an hour into the filming preparation a buzz began to develop and, into the corner of the ground came an impressive fleet of vehicles. From one of them, out stepped David Beckham. He arrived surrounded by press agents, PR agents, Adidas representatives; within minutes a small crowd had gathered watching his every move. He must have spent a few hours with us, being very agreeable to filming retakes and was generally relaxed most of the time. He filmed his piece with Freya first, then Freya stood by us and watched the training session. David then sat down for a Q&A session with the young footballers and Freya. He only had his first son Brooklyn at that point and his career was shooting up already as an England player. The fact that he was married to Posh Spice was the other fun factor.

Malc spent a fair bit of time talking to David Beckham's mum who was also there. When the filming was finished, we were due to return by coach to Lincoln.

The Adidas team had given the school an entire football kit, footballs, and Predator boots; they were going home delighted with their haul. We had been told not to ask David for autographs so I asked his PR team to send us signed pictures for the whole team, which they agreed to. As we were getting ready to go home David's mum asked if we were staying for Alex Ferguson's testimonial match that evening. We weren't, sadly but on hearing this she told Malc to wait while she spoke to David. A few minutes later she told us to wait and that they would make a plan for us to see the match. By now, the school were leaving, the BBC had wrapped up and were going so we had to trust that the next step would be OK for us! A little while later we said our goodbyes to David Beckham who had just arranged for us to have four tickets to see the match! He was a lovely shy young man who struck us even then all those years ago being like as a rich young ruler who never had much time to himself. We were chauffeur-driven to the Trafford centre where I had to buy a jacket, as I hadn't planned on staying for a match in the October night air in Manchester. After something to eat, we were taken to Old Trafford where we were given tickets to an executive seating area to watch a fantastic evening where all the great and good came to play for Alex

Fergusson. Aaron was in heaven... Malc wasn't far behind and Freya and I just loved the entire atmosphere.

The game ended and then we were chauffeur-driven home to Lincoln at David Beckham's expense.

On the way home to a house still not full of our own belongings (which were still heading back from South Africa) I looked at the twins fast asleep on our laps and heard a whisper: 'This was for your kids, keep trusting me in this adventure.'

'Thank you, God', I prayed silently 'You have spoilt us so much today. I'm so grateful my two are seeing how outrageously you can bless your children.'

Over the next few weeks we had many interviews with papers, press and local television. The school got a huge mention and Aaron remained a firm choice for the football team for the rest of the season!

We lived in Lincoln for the entire secondary school years of our twins. That was a miracle in itself; to this day it's been the longest we have lived in one house and place. The twins had done well academically and were definitely going on to further education. Our home church New Life, as it was then called, had grown significantly in those 11 years and we had made friends that we still have today.

We served the church in most departments. Malc became the youngest elder they'd had and spent the last four years as a pastor on the team. We also served an apostolic team called

Groundlevel, which enabled us to receive amazing ministry from many key leaders in the UK and beyond and in turn to have significant input to a much wider church network. We pioneered young adult programmes and served main-stage at Grapevine, the annual bible week which Groundlevel ran. It attracted thousands. Some well-known worship leaders came from this church including Chris Bowater and Jonny Markin. Sometimes we travelled together in ministry, which I considered an honour. I'm very grateful for those years of relative domestic stability and a brilliant home church that was a welcoming family of God for us all.

Higher Heights, Deeper Seas

'WHERE CAN I GO FROM YOUR SPIRIT?'

Where can I go from your spirit,
From the heavens to the depths of the sea?
Where can I go from your presence,
Knowing that your love surrounds me?

And I'm so grateful Lord
Yes, I'm so grateful Lord
To know your love is always with me
Yes, I'm so grateful Lord
You make my heart feel glad
Knowing that your love surrounds me

Lord, you have searched me and known me;
You're familiar with all of my ways.
Such is your knowledge about me
That you carefully plan all my days.

O Lord if your thoughts could be counted
They'd outnumber the grains of the sand.
Towards me, your thoughts are so precious;
Lord you know how grateful I am.

Trish Morgan, Steve Bassett
© Radical UK Music 1990

SOUTH AFRICA & THE 94.7 BIKE RACE

In 2004 Malc and I took the decision to move to South Africa. As I mentioned, we had lived there briefly five years before and our friendship with a pastor called Roelof in Johannesburg had stayed strong. Roelof was a larger than life character. He was enthusiastic and laughed loudly, had a real father's heart not just for his own family but for many more. He and his wife Carol had started their own church a few years earlier and had just acquired a new building, but the effort of doing so while the church was still a small congregation had almost burnt him out. We felt compelled to go and explore a new chapter in our lives. One thing we have realised wherever we go is that churches love to receive you and gather larger congregations, but aren't so good at letting you go when the time comes. When we told Roelof we were definitely heading his way we said in the same breath that when it was time for us to leave, 'Please send us with your blessing!'

We eventually sold our house in the UK but not before a sale fell through, leaving us only a month to pick up a new sale at a time when we had already committed to having our furniture and belongings loaded into a container to head to Johannesburg ahead of us. Sometimes these moments fill you with a mix of anxiety and self-doubt; we couldn't help wondering if we'd stepped out too far. I had a fretful week crying and worrying and then finding my composure again after I spent time praying and listening to His word.

We were sure that we had a long-term future in the beautiful country of South Africa but needed some money to be released to help us afford the first season of our arriving until we could pick up paid work.

Our twins moved out with us aged 16, along with a nephew of mine a few weeks younger called Frank.

Frank was the youngest child of one of my brothers. Every holiday he would see the twins Aaron and Freya at my parents' house as he lived in the same town, or he would come and stay with us. It was when we told him of our plans to leave for South Africa that we realised it meant a great deal to him. Frank's parents had divorced when he was young, and he was used to living half a week in one house and half a week in the other. Both parents had taken new partners and it felt to us that Frank just wanted to be in one place with one family for a while. He asked his parents if he could move with us, and, after various conversations and official paperwork, he came with us. It felt like I suddenly had triplets not twins!

Frank was well cared for financially so we had no extra burden on us... in fact when we did arrive and moved into our rented home, which was unfurnished until our goods arrived from the UK, Frank had bought himself a lovely double bed while Malc and I slept on a mattress on the floor!

I should have made a documentary about his two years with us and titled it Living with Frank. He had a naughty chuckle, and was very caring at times, but he was always late, and often losing things. He missed flights, lost his passport with his entry visa inside and whenever my phone rang, and I heard these words: 'Hello Aunty Trish; it's Frank... nightmare!' I'd get ready to hear the latest disaster!

We placed all three children into a private college to study for Cambridge 'A' levels. This was a costly decision for us. It meant we weren't able to buy a home of our own outright but we did co-invest in a lovely home with a pool. Because we lived in Johannesburg, with its high crime rate, it was on a secure 'gated' community. A visitor needed to approach the guarded gate to enter, give details of who they had come to visit and we would receive a call to give permission for entry. Once in the estate you could walk up to our house like you can in the UK; we didn't have bars on our windows, barbed wire around our fence or dogs that were trained to bark at black people... which sounds incredulous but was true in many cases. We had lived once before in Johannesburg on a corner plot off a road and had had three attempted burglaries with the last one only being foiled by armed guards arriving to chase the perpetrators away. We have friends who have been tied up and held up at gunpoint, robbed at four-way stop streets and traffic lights, and neighbours who were killed just for a cell phone. I couldn't live like that again, hence our choice of a secure estate.

Despite the violence, we really loved this rainbow nation and it was easy to make a difference almost every day. The way you spoke to non-whites was a testimony in itself. I'm in awe of many of the black and coloured community who could speak at least three languages; I knew the only difference between them and us was opportunity. We tried to empower as many as we could and, after a few years of living in Johannesburg, had a brilliant opportunity to help some young people from disadvantaged backgrounds in townships.

Hester Veltman was an extraordinary woman. She lived in Paarl near Cape Town and ran a ministry that gave disadvantaged young people a chance of an education not just in academic study or even biblical study, but in life. She would take these young adults and show them how to eat in a restaurant, read a timetable, learn to drive and manage their money. They lived in community and were called 'The Dream Team'. She also oversaw an abandoned babies refuge for babies with Aids and worked into the local townships with real joy, perseverance and anointing. By the time I knew her she had a permanent facial disfigurement from an attack when a drunk person smashed a bottle over her head and caused a bleed on her brain. Our church in Johannesburg partnered with her; after one visit to her in Paarl we began to explore the possibility of hosting the Dream Team in an urban setting for three months.

The year of 2007 saw our twins and Frank leave our house, all within two months to return for university into the UK. Our noisy, full house had emptied. It was a sudden change that took some getting used to! The option of taking a few of the Dream Team for those three months seemed natural so we hosted a beautiful young woman called Promise and her friend Olga for the time the team spent in Johannesburg.

Promise was like a mum in the team: homely, fun, encouraging, and accepting. We loved her very much. There was something so special about her and her faith.

Promise and Olga learnt how to use our washing machine after a few false starts; they learnt that cranberry jelly was for meat and not normally used as a jam for toast, and everything else in-between! We all laughed a lot and enjoyed the joy of helping them into another life! It must have seemed surreal at times to compare living in such a beautiful home to what they had previously experienced. It was like that for us too. We knew it was for a limited time and we happily shared our blessings with these two girls and held what God had provided for us lightly.

The Dream Team served the church really well, helping to develop the youth. When time came for them to leave, we suggested Promise should be able to return once her course had finished, to serve as a receptionist at the church. This she did, but only after Malc and I had left to live in Northern Ireland. We kept in touch and watched her blossom into a fine young woman of God. A few years later she trained to be a teacher, got a job at a really good school, married, fell pregnant but tragically lost a baby close to full term. Her husband and her went through the grief and heartbreak with real faith and dignity and later had a beautiful daughter and twin boys, who they adore. We recently met up again in Greece on a ministry trip.

We love going on journeys with people and seeing them become what God intended them to be: men and women of significance and purpose.

The Barn Church grew exponentially during our time with them. One major cultural breakthrough moment came when we introduced a coffee break halfway through the service. We had noticed that new people came just before the start of the service and often left quickly at the end too. Let me digress a minute; if you ever want to do a talk to churches do it on the way they treat visitors. We've experienced many forms regarding this issue. When on sabbatical once, we went to Malaysia and Singapore where In their churches, as a visitor, you are seated near the front and given a badge saying VIP; you are welcomed in the service and invited afterwards to a special coffee room to meet pastors and the welcome team. Recently we attended a church in the UK where we weren't greeted at all, not even during the 'turn to somebody new and say hello' section. We waited to the end of the service which was ending with ministry and left via their coffee shop which had no one serving and small pockets of people chatting to each other with no one looking like they were ready to meet and greet new people. I'm not saying there is only one correct way to treat visitors, but some churches are just un-thinking in how to be more welcoming to visitors.

What works in one country may not work in another. You have to know the culture of the country. We were fairly confident that taking a break in the service while the kids were going out to their classes anyway would work to give new people a genuine ten minutes to say 'Hi' and make a connection with some existing members. We did this by allocating six coffee stations around the church with one dedicated to new people. We met with some resistance; having coffee wasn't deemed spiritual enough for some, but we took the risk and it was just the breakthrough we needed. The congregation loved the idea and we began to grow quickly. Our worship team grew too; we had some incredibly talented worship musicians join the church and soon we were having powerful and anointed services. It was wonderful.

The other huge cultural shift we made was centred on community involvement.

Every year, the city of Johannesburg held a bike race through the city and suburbs called the '94.7K bike race'. It was named after a popular national radio station.

It attracted thousands of participants and raised hundreds of thousands of South African Rands for charity. There was only one snag – it was being held on a Sunday.

We were taking a coffee one morning, the first year we were in Johannesburg, in a shopping mall not far from our church not long after the race. In the coffee shop we read a notice from the race organisers apologising to the local businesses and churches for any disruption they may have caused.

We chatted to the owner of the coffee shop, who wasn't at all bothered by the disruption ... his son rode in the race and he said, 'What's one day in a year when it's all for a good cause?' Sadly, this was not the view of some local churches. They had complained that they members couldn't get to their services due to police road closures and that they couldn't hear themselves sing hymns while the noise from the race went on! Hence the letter of apology that was being sent out. To be honest, we were embarrassed. Here was the church, the agent for change, something that was supposed to be salt and light and loving people grumbling and complaining instead. We asked for the letter, took it to our leadership team and suggested we do something in the opposite spirit. We suggested our church supported the race event the following year and offer to help.

The ensuing leadership discussions got very lively. One suggestion was that, because the race started so early in the morning (6:00am) due to it being in November, we could start our service later, having some members go down to the race to cheer them on. Another suggestion was for half the church to go to the race while the others stayed to pray! And what about the offering?

We strongly argued for the church to SHUT ITS DOORS, go down to the race route and cheer the riders on together... to make some noise and get involved. Praise God, Roelof, the senior pastor agreed.

We contacted the race organisers to discuss our suggestion of being involved. I wish we had recorded it.

'Hello is that the race organisers of the 94.7?'

'Yes, who's speaking,' answered a lady on the other end of the phone.

'We are phoning on behalf of a local church which is on the route for the 94.7 race in Honeydew and we are wondering how we can help next year'. There was a silence on the end of the phone. Then the voice said, 'Sorry, did you say help?'

'Yes' we replied. 'We want to come and support something that blesses the city and help out.' Once the organisers had got over the shock that we were not complaining but offering our services, they came to see us to discuss how we could help. 'I haven't been in a church in ten years' said one of the women... as she walked through our building. They were blown away with our thinking and told us we were the first church in the entire city to offer our support.

They agreed to give us a spectator zone and said we would be allowed to hold out wet sponges that the riders could grab to cool down with as they cycled past. We had actually done a recce and chosen the stretch for the zone, it was a narrower part of the course, slightly uphill, where we felt riders would need encouragement and we would also have a longer time to be noticed by them!

When we shared it with the church there was instantly a buzz of excitement.

We had teams spring up in our church to help make it happen. Some wanted to race, some to have a small bike repair stop, others wanted to braai (which is like a BBQ) and give away hot dogs. The band were getting ready to play from the back of a lorry from 6am till 1pm as that's how long it would take for all the riders to come past! The rest of the church would cheer, clap, sing and encourage the riders on their way.

When the morning came, the first group of us were at the race site by 5 am; it was summer after all so it was daylight and pleasantly warm. At around six, suddenly helicopters whirled overhead, cars, police and TV crew cars raced past as the professional riders flew past us in a peloton.

While still setting up we were suddenly aware of a motorbike that came and stopped by us. A big guy walked up to us and began chatting. Within seconds we recognised him, Jeremy

Mansfield, the breakfast presenter of the hugely popular 94.7 radio station morning programme.

'Gee'... he said. 'You guys – what's the plan?' We explained our story and he was astounded. 'A church? Closing your service to support the Race? Good on ya.' He stopped for photos then got back on his bike, and off he went.

The race was a huge success; we had only a few hundred in the church at that point but most came to the roadside. We branded ourselves in T-shirts and caps but forbade anyone from handing out bible tracts. Our presence would be our witness. Sure enough, as the riders went through, they looked at us in amazement. Who were all these cheering people? Who was the band who were playing a mix of pop songs and worship material? Some stopped for help with their bikes or took sponges. From the race organisers to the many participants, we heard nothing but thanks.

By the end of the day I hardly had a voice, and couldn't clap anymore, or play or sing another note. We flopped into our chairs at the end of the day, elated. Our church community were buzzing but the best was yet to come.

On Monday morning on his national radio show Jeremy Mansfield gave a big shout out to the church that closed its doors to support the race and provided an awesome atmosphere to the race... he named us on air and our phones immediately started to ring.

Over the following Sundays we began to have families arrive asking 'Are you guys the 94.7 church?' They hadn't thought of God much until that point but that experience as they raced through had made them want to find the church that got involved in the community in such a fun way.

Malc and I personally befriended several couples directly from the race and over time we ran an Alpha course and helped them find a living and real faith in Jesus. For the record, the offering that month in our church exceeded its normal monthly amount! You can't out-give God either in any of time, talent or treasure.

BELFAST DAYS

ADRIAN

The rain was not just falling heavily; at one point it was coming horizontally at me, and there was a real howling wind as we jumped into our church office early in January to re-open after the Christmas break.

It was one year since we had left Johannesburg and taken over leading City Church in Belfast. It was a church we had actually worshipped in fifteen years earlier. It was a relatively young church but it had already had quite a history of struggle particularly with leadership. We thought we knew what we had said yes to and still didn't regret taking this step to minister in the church. It was, however, immensely challenging with the first task being to find a common vision that most of the church could gather round.

Part of what we inherited was a rather unreliable caretaker. Davey was a bit of a chancer. He didn't clean very well and, after a few days of our returning in January he hadn't turned up to work. We got on with cleaning the church ourselves including the toilets, which I found myself having to do on a regular basis anyway, while Malc went round Davey's house looking for him. The back door to his rented flat was still open but he had disappeared. The shadow of paramilitary activity hasn't gone away from Belfast, it still remains in the stauncher areas of the city and, if you have done something against the local 'gangs', you often had to make yourself scarce. The only reason we found out where Davey had gone was that he phoned a few weeks later to ask about his pay-check! He was hiding in Glasgow at a men's hostel using a false name – we never saw him again.

At the same time a letter had been pushed under our office door, Malc opened it, read it, put it down and carried on. Being a bit nosey I asked him what it was about. The letter was from a guy offering to volunteer in any capacity in the church. Looking at the address we noticed he was on probation release from prison. Maybe if we'd still had Davey we wouldn't have thought about it, but I was getting a bit fed up of having to be cleaner alongside the other roles I undertook so I suggested Malc meet him at least to see if this guy would be suitable to help us out. Malc had to be persuaded... but he arranged to meet this guy a few days later in Common Grounds – our amazing coffee shop next door, and take it from there.

'I have just met one of the most wonderful, gentle guy in years.' said Malc on his return from the meeting. He excitedly retold me the story this young man had told him hours earlier. He had been sentenced to a long-term prison sentence for a crime he committed as a teenager while high on drugs, a crime about which he was deeply remorseful and ashamed.

In prison he had met some folk from the prison fellowship and, over a few years had started to read his bible. While still inside he had made a commitment to follow Jesus. He was then discipled by these lovely people in weekly meetings and his faith had grown. Now out and living in a halfway house, he was desperate to use his time wisely, stay away from trouble and bad friends, and make a fresh start. Only if he was working Monday to Friday would the prison authorities agree to his partial release – he had to return to prison every weekend.

Malc took it to our leaders and, within the week, Adrian began to volunteer for us. Sure enough, Adrian was a gentle man, he laughed heartily at things and you could never have imagined such a past in what was now a truly transformed life.

After he was eventually released and allowed to return to his family home, we employed him; he was an absolute joy to have in the church. He would clean with worship music blasting from the main speakers and was valued way beyond what he did, as a loving brother in our community.

One sore point was he was a supporter of Manchester United football club; as Liverpool supporters it provided lots of banter, but hey, we overlooked this for once!

A few years later, Adrian married a young woman in our church. We married them at our church camp in Rostrevor in 2011 and today they have three lovely boys.

One Saturday, not long after his wedding, Malc got a phone call out of the blue from a sensation-grabbing local Sunday tabloid simply informing us they were running a story about

Adrian and his ex-cell-mate (his friend who was also with us now in church) and wondering what the congregation would think if they knew of his wicked past? Malc made one statement about the church fully knowing his past and that it was a story of redemption and reformation and there was nothing else to say.

We waited apprehensively for the next morning and sure enough not only was it the main headline on the front page but his story filled more pages in the paper. The headline used was 'Killers at the altar!' The other headlines were just as bad, and featured photos taken from his Facebook page. Adrian and his new wife were mortified and changed their phone numbers and Facebook page. They went into hiding for a short while. If the purpose of the story was to create disgust, alienation and vindictiveness, it produced the opposite. Our community church protected them, loved them and cared for them beautifully; one man walked into the coffee shop with an envelope of money to thank our church for being such an accepting community and helping these young men turn their lives around!

The newspaper delved into his imprisonment and the crime he had committed but totally ignored his life afterwards. We had phone calls and letters of encouragement from both Northern Ireland churches and further afield. Adrian continues living a transformed life to this day. Officers from the probation service of Northern Ireland were brilliant in helping him adjust to life outside and we worked closely with them as he re-built his life.

A final instalment in this story is that, many months later, a professional photographer came to us after church one Sunday and said with a wicked smile 'Just thought you'd like to know I charged the paper for using my photos in the article without permission and I've put the money into the offering.' We couldn't stop laughing – what a life this was.

We had the most incredible time leading City Church. Through various events we found ourselves working with the police, councillors, MPs, the city council and residents' committees.

The 'Holylands' area of Belfast is where City Church is located. It houses several thousand University students in narrow terraced streets. Every St Patrick's Day the students would have an all-day street party with lots of drinking. Thousands of other young adults join them for the day and it would all get a bit manic. The party would usually start around 10.00am and continue until early evening. when they would re-locate to the city's many bars and clubs. The first year Malc and I arrived in Belfast the event turned nasty and violent; there were skirmishes between students and police, causing £30,000 of damage to the surrounding streets. Bottles were thrown at the police and the riot squad were needed to quell the situation. After this I started a glass bottle campaign to remove those offensive weapons from our locality with support from local councillors. The next year we asked to meet with police and city council with a novel plan. We offered to 'patrol' the streets of Holylands and collect empty beer cans and bottles in large wheelie bins to take away the possibility of them being used in violent brawls or skirmishes with the police. During this time, we said we would engage the students with low key banter and help to keep the peace as best as we could. The police agreed providing they could use our church as a 'base' should things escalate badly again.

During the day we filled dozens of Eurobins, and the recycling lorries came every few hours to take away these bins while the police stayed in our church hall and relaxed as the day went off peacefully and happily! It was so successful and started a great relationship between the community, police, the city council and the church. Our 'street-pastors' have been used every year since. We couldn't believe how many bins were filled in a day but we so enjoyed walking the streets chatting with students and helping keep the atmosphere happy and friendly. Regular meetings would be held in our coffee shop after this between the police, council and residents to help maintain good relationships.

RACE HATE RESCUE

In 2009 our church took in over 100 Roma folk overnight after local youths had threatened to firebomb their houses to make them leave the area. They had been throwing stones and breaking windows; the Roma were too scared to return to their homes. One of our church members worked in the community and phoned to ask if we could help shelter these families until the police could calm the situation and maybe move them elsewhere. We had 15 minutes to give an answer as the threat was escalating. We simply said yes. Some of our guys had been cleaning up at the church after some building work had just finished so they offered to help get the church ready and some other church members turned up with food and blankets to help.

Within 30 minutes the first police van had turned up and out came 15 Roma, followed by more vans until we seemed to have a tide of humanity pouring into our church building, including frightened, upset and young children crying and looking bewildered. Within a few hours it became apparent they would have to stay the night.

Fortunately, our church has removable chairs and a large space the families could use. It was around 10pm and the kids were watching cartoons on our big screen, when the Red Cross started bringing in blankets and neighbours were arriving with food to share. By now we had many more than the original 100, as their relatives from other parts of the city turned up all discussing what had happened and asking what was going to happen next. It was very noisy but calm as they knew they were in a safe place. The city mayor, Naomi Long, turned up with large plates of food for the Roma and a local landlord went and collected 20 mattresses from his flats to provide bedding.

The story as it unfolded attracted main news groups and the next morning, before we knew it, we were under siege from outside broadcasting vans and journalists.

I had previously worked in a local news gathering production team so wasn't too fazed by the media scrum. Having said that, it was definitely an intense and a fast-moving situation. For the next 24 hours Malc, I and other staff were being interviewed by the BBC, CNN, ITV, SKY news and loads of local and national radio stations and journalists. By the end of the next day, a local leisure centre had been commandeered to take the families and they all left.

A week after the initial story was dying down our church building was attacked, with bricks thrown through our windows. Straight away the media came back to cover part two of the drama. This time we had a lot of political interest and, at one point we were invited to listen to a voicemail on behalf of the local UVF offering their services to find out who the perpetrators were and bring them to justice. We declined that offer; then we were told Martin McGuinness wanted to visit and meet us, so we agreed to let him visit. We were a 'protestant' church but had striven to be open to all expressions of Christian faith, and some of our congregation were doing incredible behind-the-scenes work with mixed communities and paramilitaries. Still, the initial suggestion of Martin McGuinness visiting made us think twice. He was now deputy first minister and seemed to have left his military past in the

IRA, but his associations with these groups were still concerning to say the least.

The church and coffee shop were closed whilst we dealt with the crisis. When he arrived, he was with the Mayor of Belfast – a lady we had already met. We sat in the coffee shop discussing the previous week's events, the attack on the church and our response. Martin was an incredible, gentle man. He listened well, didn't seem to be in a hurry and was warm and very polite.

Then we were asked to do a press conference. So, out on the church steps in front of broken glass doors and windows, Malc found himself standing next to Martin McGuinness and Naomi Long, giving a press conference.

The message in Northern Ireland of working together, standing up to intimidation and working across the divide remains the same today as it did that sunny afternoon when Malc, the Mayor and Martin McGuinness held their press conference. Little did I know I was to meet him again in a surreal moment a few years later in Belfast.

THAT HANDSHAKE!

In 2012 the talk in Belfast was all about the Queen's visit to Northern Ireland. She had agreed to meet Martin McGuinness face to face and shake his hand in a line-up of dignitaries as she was re-opening the Lowry theatre in Stranmillis, half a mile away from our church and offices.

The radio stations were airing differing opinions and suggestions were coming from hard-line Catholic communities and some of his own party Sinn Fein that this was a sell-out by McGuinness.

For some reason Malc wasn't in Belfast. As I was on my own in the office, I decided I would walk across to see the Queen arrive before she went inside the theatre.

How naive I was! I wasn't even allowed to walk down nearby streets. Huge police vehicles had closed the streets around and declared several square miles around the theatre a 'sterile zone' – security speak for keeping everything undesirable out!

I hung around with the press corps for a while until a commanding officer marched up and ordered us even further back down the street. It meant you'd need a zoom camera to even catch a glimpse of her Majesty! Rather forlornly I turned to leave. I wanted to go back through the local park, but even this was now locked as her arrival was imminent. Helicopters were flying overhead as I decided just to walk back to the church office the long way round on the main roads. I was on my own; no traffic was allowed and as I was about to pass the front of the Ulster Museum, two unmarked cars pulled up just ahead of me. They stopped (on double yellow lines!) and a plain-clothes policeman stood in front of me and said: 'Clear' into the lapel microphone on his coat.

For one moment I thought it might have been the queen, but out stepped Martin McGuinness who was being taken to a safe house just a half a mile away from the theatre about to hold this historic meeting. The next few minutes were beyond surreal, but I felt it was a God-given opportunity I wasn't going to miss.

'Martin' I shouted and he turned to meet me, 'I just want to wish you well for what you're doing today' I went on to encourage him for this historical moment. He was so appreciative that he actually didn't stop shaking my hand, which I found quite funny. I think he was really nervous and thanked me so much for the kind words. I'm not sure what else I said but I did finish by saying I'd let him go as he had a more important hand to shake than mine!

The security ushered him into the house and like that he was gone and I carried on my walk back to the office. As I did, I got my phone out to call Malc thinking he was not going to believe what had just happened. At that moment, I felt the incredible presence of God right next to me. I sensed my diversion had been God-ordained and I wondered if God had used me to say a few words to a national leader moments before an historic moment took place – wow. I felt very strange and deeply humbled. In these moments you do wonder, 'What is going to happen next and what else might God want from me?'

MID 8: I BELIEVE IN MIRACLES

While living in Belfast and leading City Church we discovered that the church was coming up to 21 years of being in existence. We felt it was hugely significant. A church, which had had its beginnings among students and young people was coming of age. We made a plan to host a celebratory weekend to mark this milestone.

In the back of an office filing cabinet, we discovered the original covenant document that had legally established the church. We actually recognised three out of the four signatories but not the last one, who was called Noel Gilmour.

We were trying to put a face to the name as it sounded familiar but we couldn't place him and so shut the folder, put it away and left it at that.

A couple of days after our discovery, Malc and I decided to go on a long walk along the Belfast Lough coast. We walked from St. Helen's Bay to Bangor and, as is pretty normal for UK weather, we started out in sunshine and ended in a significant rainstorm. We were soaked to the skin and feeling very cold, so we walked up the high street in Bangor and jumped into the first coffee shop we could find.

I sat down shivering as Malc stood in a long queue to order coffee. After a little while I became aware of a couple looking at me, I didn't recognise them so just ignored them.

Suddenly, this couple walked straight up to me, and asked outright if my name was Trish Morgan.

I replied it was, then they asked me if I used to sing in the band Heartbeat. I nodded my head and said yes...

'Well, you won't remember us, but a few years ago we hosted some of your team members when you did some concerts in Lurgan town where we used to live,' said the man. I could remember the event well, Malc and I had only just got married and we had really enjoyed our visit to Northern Ireland.

At this point Malc came back with my much-needed hot drink, and joined in with the conservation; and after a few minutes we asked their names. 'I'm Noel Gilmour and this is my wife Liz'.

'What? You're Noel Gilmour!' I jumped up out of my seat in astonishment. My response took him by surprise but we began to tell him the story of finding his signature only a few days earlier and how unexpected it was that now we were meeting him. All the more incredible was the fact that they were just visiting Bangor that morning and they didn't live in the town either. None of us had a pen or paper or a phone on us which was very strange so Malc gave them a contact card he had in his back pocket and asked them to call us to have another catch up at some point. We both agreed this seemed to be a divine re-introduction and were intrigued as to what would happen next.

We met up again a week later, and over the next few years Noel and Liz became great friends and re-connected with our local church; even after we left City Church, they stayed in touch supporting us in prayer, finance and friendship.

When we started our charity, Noel was an easy choice to ask to become a trustee and he and Liz visited Greece on a regular basis.

Then, in September 2018 we took a call from Noel. It was a sudden tragic turn of events involving his son Matthew who was 31 years old.

Matthew was taking part in a mountain bike race through Tollymore Forest Park in Northern Ireland. He had been on a practice run the day before but had had an accident and collided with a tree at great speed. He had been knocked unconscious; a fellow biker who had heard the crash called the St John's ambulance crew who were attending the event and arrived within minutes. They quickly realised it was very serious and an air ambulance was called to rush him to The Royal Victoria Hospital in Belfast. This was time-critical as Matt had sustained a severe head injury. The air ambulance was actually not too far away having attended another incident so they quickly picked him up and Matthew's fight for life began.

When Noel spoke to us, he was obviously in shock and extremely distressed. He asked us to join them in prayer. We were in Greece so pray was all we could do. We began with others to cry out to God to save Matthew's life.

A few days later the medical diagnosis and prognosis was bleak. He had severe diffuse axonal injuries to his brain, fractured neck vertebrae, and a broken eye socket. By far the most serious problem was the amount of time he had been without oxygen before the medics arrived.

The doctors told Noel and Liz that, if he survived, his life would be very dramatically different due to reduced brain function and there would be considerable doubt about his ability to walk or do any basic functions himself. Matthew was single, so any future caring would fall back on Noel and Liz.

They and many others knew that it would take a miracle, so we all began to pray for that. First, we prayed for Matthew to come out of his deep coma after the surgery they had performed, then we prayed that, as he recovered, he would have full brain function and limb movement restored. Noel, Liz and his close family surrounded Matt's bedside with music, prayer, worship and ordinary chat. They barely slept for weeks themselves as the tension and stress rose to peak levels. With something like this it's a fine balancing act of faith and fear, managing realistic expectations but also fusing the atmosphere with hope in a miracle-working God.

Within weeks they had their first breakthrough, the brain swelling began to come down and he was transferred to a neurology ward. For a while they induced a coma and he had a tracheostomy to aid the ventilation.   Five weeks later Matthew slowly awoke. First, he began to move his arms and legs, and then he opened his eyes. He could recognise the family's faces and slowly but surely began to communicate. Relief, joy and thankfulness began to flow. If God could do this much, then surely, with prayer and the medical team's help Matthew could possibly walk again and fully recover.

We were back in the UK in November, eight weeks after the accident, and Matt had just left The Royal in Belfast to move to a rehabilitation hospital near to where Noel and Liz lived. We were privileged to visit him during that time and thrilled to see him borrow his sister's mobile phone and use it to talk to a friend.

A few months later, Matthew returned to his parents' home and gradually back to his own house. After a few months he returned part-time to his old job working in a garage – not as a mechanic to begin with, as his strength wasn't up to speed but he got there, and eventually Matt recovered so well he got back his driving licence and a full-on life.

HOW GREAT IS OUR GOD?

I can't to this day understand why sometimes we ask for a miracle and don't seem to get it. There are some equally heart-breaking stories of little ones dying and not recovering and yet this one coming through so wonderfully. But it will never stop us from praying for the miracle to happen, as ultimately it is God's call not ours.

BRIDGE

'Take your everyday, ordinary life, your sleeping, eating, going to work and walking around life, and place it before God as an offering.'

Romans 12: The Message

FRIENDSHIP, FAITH AND BIG PRAYERS

MARIA

While staying in Liverpool, but knowing we would soon be moving to Greece, we had a message from Freya's boyfriend living in York – he asked if he could come to see us. It felt more than a casual visit as he was coming alone; sure enough, Gavin asked us if he could marry our beautiful daughter. By some crazy coincidence his home was Newtonards, the next town to Belfast, and he would have only been a few miles away from us had we stayed in Northern Ireland! He and Freya had met and fallen in love in York where both of them had gone to university. We were happy for them both and left them to plan and organise a wedding the following year. We caught up with them occasionally to work out all the practical requirements and help keep the big day as stress-free as possible. Gavin's dad had become seriously ill and it was a bitter-sweet moment for them to encounter such a backdrop to what is meant to be a happy day so early in their lives.

In the October half term Freya flew out to see us in our basic furnished apartment in Greece. We loved her visit and it gave us a chance to discuss wedding plans. One of our Greek contacts in Athens mentioned that she had recently spent some time with a woman who ran a wedding business from her home near Chalkida and suggested that maybe Freya and I would like to meet her. Well, why not? We weren't exactly busy or spoilt for choice when it came to friends and I felt this would be a good first contact with a local Greek woman.

The first challenge was making a plan to meet Maria, the name of the lady; when she called she was quite sure we wouldn't find her home in a nearby village so she suggested we meet at the bus station in Chalkida. Between her broken English and my learner's Greek we made a plan, and a few days later we managed to meet up.

Maria was a beautiful woman from the beginning, inside and out. She was youthful, with an olive skin, brown eyes and a welcoming smile and she took us to her home. The house was a double-story house with an enclosed garden and a Greek flag flying proudly outside. Her father had built it for her and her sister Peggy and they shared the floors with their husbands and children.

The first thing you realise in Greece is you rarely meet a person alone the first time! Especially until they get to know you, they will always have someone else there. It could be the mother, sister or cousin but this time it was with an equally attractive friend called Stavroula. The business was wedding stationery, favours and the decorating of venues.

We were welcomed in and looked around the displays while Maria kept disappearing in and out of the room. She was making us coffee but somehow kept forgetting things and so our flow of conversation was stilted till we were all sat down and began discussing the differences between a Greek wedding and a UK one... believe me, there are many! It wasn't until Stavroula asked Freya if she was going to have an Orthodox wedding that a fascinating conversation began. Firstly, Maria's friend was astonished that we weren't Orthodox – 'what else is there?' she asked?

At this point it might be helpful to know that Greece has had a turbulent history and that the one thing that the Greeks feel after suffering from the Ottoman Empire days has been the constant presence of their Orthodox church. The culture is enmeshed into their faith and family, and they are taught that anything outside of Orthodoxy is heresy. I understood Stavroula's reaction but since she asked...

Freya explained how the Christian faith had many expressions in the UK and she was part of a very modern church plant from an established church of England in York. As Freya went on, the difference between the two girls was striking. Stavroula was bewildered, while Maria was nodding and smiling and her eyes were sparkling.

I was aware through my contact in Athens that Maria had recently had a long conversation about faith and my friend from Athens had prayed with her. But this was our first meeting and the culture isn't one where you go in too deep too fast, so we left the conversation there. We ordered some Greek honey wedding favours, thanked them for their hospitality and left.

As we waved goodbye Freya and I drove off chatting about the visit and prayed that I would soon meet Maria again as she had seemed so open. I didn't have long to wait!

It was Freya's last evening with us, and rather than go into town along the beautiful waterfront for something to eat we chose to stay local and try out a restaurant in our neighbourhood.

We arrived early for Greeks (8pm) and we were the first in. We were offered a table by the window. This is Greece at its finest; the Greeks love their food and it's an incredible social time where no one is in a hurry. Once sat at a table, no one is going to hurry you off in a few hours unless it's a high holiday!

We had only just had our starter course when Freya said, 'Mum, I think I can see Maria and another lady across the road in a park with some children'

'I wouldn't have thought so,' I replied. 'It's nearly 9pm and she lives 8 kilometres away – surely the kids would be in bed?' But Freya was adamant it was, I looked out and sure enough there was Maria with another friend and their kids playing on the swings.

We told Malc to stay at the table in case the waiter thought we were leaving without paying while we went out.

We walked across to the park. Maria's face was a picture, and mine probably was too! After a brief chat, we discovered this was her very first trip to this park but that her friend lived nearby. She had no idea where we lived but was amazed to meet us again so soon! That was it, twice in one day and after our earlier prayer there was no way I was going to leave it as a 'coincidence' so I said to her:

'Maria, I believe this is God allowing us to meet twice in one day'

'Yes', she said, 'so do I!'

'So, my friend, let's meet for coffee next week'

'Absolutely' she replied!From that moment we began a journey of friendship and faith together. Maria regularly met up with me so we could look at the bible and various YouTube teaching clips to help her learn and understand about Jesus. Slowly she grew in her faith in between her busy family life and the classic non-diarising of Greek life. It wasn't uncommon for Malc to be told the night before of a staff meeting the next morning or a parents' evening that day. Over time, Maria and her husband opened their house to Malc and myself and we met her sister Peggy, who was married to Tassos; they lived in the apartment above. Maria's family and all the children lived constantly in each other's homes with a real extended family feel. She was the first disciple of our work and, within a year, her witness had influenced others to enquire about Jesus with some making commitments to follow God and join our young community.

PEGGY

A few years had gone by and our community was growing slowly. Not for us the tens but the ones and twos over many months of meeting for coffee, sharing our home for meals and, at some point asking if they would be interested in looking at some DVDs explaining about the Christian faith more deeply. The DVD in question was the original version of Alpha, with Nicky Gumbel sharing stories about Princess Diana and the fashion sense of all the audience being really dated. But THANK GOD for Alpha, what a blessed course for evangelism it has become!

At every church we've pastored at, we have introduced it and led many people to Jesus through it. Thank you Lord for Holy Trinity Church Brompton and their provision of Alpha to the church. The reason we had these versions was because it was the only version which had been accurately subtitled in Greek – believe me we've had some howlers in our community using Google translate or YouTube translate when things are not properly subtitled!

It was autumn when Peggy, Maria's sister, said she was interested in doing the course. I should say at this point I don't think you can ever run a ten-week course in Greece concurrently - it's impossible! Even a four-week course would only work over a longer period of time, they simply cannot make such a commitment, anything can happen from one week to the next and you would be left with either an entirely different set of people or no one at all! We did once try a marriage course. We invited friends over from the UK to help us and, with Eleni's amazing translating skills and input, we thought we had a great course for our community and friends. We decided to run it over three nights and a Sunday in the same week. The first night surprised us with a great turn-out, but by the end of the week we were struggling to get the same couples back or even both out for the session; on the final evening several couples brought their kids! Our dear friends were ripping up their course book notes as fast as they could, adapting it to try and be relevant to our lovely group of people, and they were very gracious in their participation. They left having learnt a very quick lesson in how to adapt when ministering in a very different culture.

Because Peggy worked at a supermarket, she wasn't free until after 9.30pm at night, so I was leaving my home to get to her apartment for a 10pm start. Maria and Peggy would be in their loungewear or pyjamas, and it was often midnight by the time I left to come home. The course ran through until Christmas and some of those nights were very cold and dark.

One evening in November, I arrived at the house to find a visibly upset Peggy.

She worked for the supermarket chain Carrefour; it hadn't been managed well in recent years and had become a failing business. As deputy manager, Peggy had been called into the office and asked to begin to draw up lists of which staff to be made redundant with immediate effect, followed by a list that could possibly stay on until Christmas. This request had sent her into a spin, as she tearfully told me. How could she tell staff that just before Christmas they were being made redundant?

I said we should pray about this situation, but before we prayed, I asked who she would like to take over the supermarket chain. Without hesitation she replied 'Sklavanitis', a family-led supermarket chain. But she said, they were only based in Athens – not all over Greece.

'Yet!' I replied. 'God knows these workers need to keep their jobs. Some were the only workers in the whole family and, even though €2.50 an hour wasn't much of a salary, no-one would want to lose their jobs, let alone just before Christmas.

'So, let's pray for this company to take over your store!' Peggy nodded but Maria's eyes were now very large and her whole body-language told me she thought I was crazy to pray like this. Shutting one's eyes is highly recommended when praying big crazy prayers... it blocks out the unbelief for starters and helps you concentrate on the one who answers prayer! I simply asked for this company to take over from Carrefour... and as soon as possible as we didn't want anyone to lose their jobs. Amen.

We made coffee and settled down to another chapter of Alpha. I left after midnight and went home. The following week I arrived; this time Peggy was a mix of delirious disbelief and shock. Maria was hovering around her in the kitchen; to begin with I was trying to read the atmosphere as to what was going on. My Greek was still at best average but I quickly picked up the fact that something very unusual was unfolding. As I arrived Peggy had been receiving a call from her area manager. Unbeknown to her, Sklavanitis had been in secret talks with the Carrefour chain for the past six months and, subject to Government agreement on competition rules were making a bid not just for her store but the entire chain of stores throughout Greece – BOOM! Now the girls were getting excited, chatting, hugging, crying and walking around saying, 'It's a miracle... but I don't believe!' They were saying it in repeated cycles. WOW! To be honest I was also amazed. I'm not sure I'd seen a big prayer of this kind ever answered so rapidly but said to the girls: 'I CAN believe it... we SHOULD believe the prayers we pray can be heard and answered. But I'm amazed like you as to how quickly this has come about. Thank you, Jesus!' We all hugged and laughed and I got Peggy to thank God for his answer to our prayer.

Peggy is like many people we meet in Greece in that her faith was usually in the background. It comes to the fore during Easter, Christmas and baby baptisms but apart from that there are gaps in their understanding of who Jesus is and how you can have a relationship with God and learn to talk to Him and hear back. It is only once you have that relationship that the Holy Spirit becomes your guide and gives you the power to live a transformed life. Sometimes it's a matter of joining up the dots for them. So here we were, with a lesson in prayer demonstrated and an answer so astonishing that it was beyond anything we could ask or think! After all the excitement we watched another chapter of Alpha and at the end I said my goodnights.

It would have been the most tempting thing to say. 'Now you have had your answer to prayer let's push for a prayer of repentance and confession,' but I knew it wouldn't take long for Peggy to come to that place herself. I left that night so happy, so mind-blown about this journey of faith we were on and the way these personal testimonies would never be taken away from these women. A few weeks later Peggy prayed out loud dedicating her life to Jesus to become a follower of Him and a few months later she was promoted to become manageress of the whole store. It was time to party!

LOVED

Loved - on the day I came to be
Loved – You're still watching over me
Loved – as you see the days go by
There's love everlasting 'til I die
There's love everlasting 'til I die

Amazing, energising love
Washes over me, washes over me
Amazing, motivating love
Washes over me, washes over me.

Accepting, all-embracing love
Washes over me, washes over me
Accepting, all forgiving love
Washes over me, washes over me

'Cause I'm loved on the day I came to be
Loved – You're still watching over me
Loved – as you see the years go by
There's love everlasting,
Love everlasting, love everlasting

Trish & Aaron Morgan
© Radical UK Music 2005

SYRIAN LOVE STORY

KARAM

In the first year of our time in Greece a civil war began in Syria. Geographically Greece is not that far from the Middle East and at times when we have been living in Greece you feel this merging of culture between the western European countries and the Middle Eastern ones. Some of the practices, family ties and official documents have more of a Middle Eastern feel. Indeed, the calendar Greece follows is the Julian calendar, not the Gregorian one, often leaving us to celebrate Easter and other holiday times at different dates to the Western world.

Elias and Voula lived in Athens and were long-time friends of my parents. They had begun a refugee support work to help Syrian refugees in the early days of the civil war. Initially I would travel to Athens every week to support them as they began to be inundated with frantic phone calls in Arabic from relatives and associates. Elias was born in Syria but many years ago had come to live in Greece. Soon the ones and twos became tens and twenties, mainly young professional men escaping the civil war and army call-ups. They were engineers, architects, computer programmers, dentists, and teachers: often excellent English speakers and we were highly impressed with their politeness and behaviour. Both Malc and I tried to help where we could but our city was a 150-kilometre round trip to Athens which limited our availability. Occasionally our friends would travel to us in Chalkida, often on a Sunday, where we would have fellowship times and lunches together. On one of these days Karam walked into our lives.

It was just before the first Christmas we were in Greece and I was asked to sing at a special meal our friends were hosting in Athens for refugee families, in conjunction with another well-established ministry.

I agreed to sing some of my songs, feeling very aware they were not Middle Eastern in sound or in Arabic but hey... I tried!

After people had spoken and I had sung it was time for the food, the hall was crammed with at least a few hundred refugees. By now the refugees in Greece weren't just young men but entire families and it was chaotic. Many were sleeping in tents at various parks around Athens and relying on charitable groups for food and support.

I was invited to stay for the meal but was concerned about the time and I didn't want to leave so late to catch my bus back, I also couldn't see where to sit at any table. I chose to go into the balcony, balancing my plate of chicken and rice on my lap. I sat near another woman in her Arabic dress and hijab, her baby and a young man. We got talking but the noise downstairs was so loud I could hardly hear them. Still the introduction was interesting enough!

'Hello, I'm Trish and I'm from a city near Athens, lovely to meet you... what's your name?'

The woman didn't speak any English but smiled and nodded but then the young man leant over and said in good English that his name was Karam and he was 26 (the same age as my twins Aaron and Freya). I repeated my introduction. He smiled and said: 'I know who you are, in fact I've been to your house!' I was totally amazed!

'How have you been to my house? I live 75 kilometres away!' He smiled and told me that the week before Malc and I had invited anyone we knew to our house for mulled wine and mince pies. Elias had brought four men with him from Athens and he had been one of them!

It was true we had invited our entire apartment block, some of Malc's teaching colleagues, my neighbours, Maria and a few other friends from Athens but I honestly had never met Karam that evening, so we began chatting further.

He said he had stayed with the small group of Syrian men that evening and not socialised with others; even thinking about that made me smile, a group of refugee men mixing with local Greeks, just as it should be but in reality, almost unheard of. I'm so glad they felt welcomed in my home.

Meanwhile, back in the moment, the hall by now was so full I didn't want to stay any longer, so I said my goodbyes, went downstairs to say goodbye to the others and began trying to navigate my way to the exit. Just as I was leaving Karam came back to me, took me by the hand and looked straight into my eyes...

'Please don't forget me,' he said. Instantly he had my attention and I felt something connect inside.

'I won't' I replied. That evening when I got home I told Malc I had met a young Syrian man that I believed God had brought to us to help, look after and support.

A few weeks went by and it was New Year. Some of our furniture had finally been shipped out to our home and we needed help upon its arrival. I called Elias and asked if Karam could come and help us. We would put him up overnight, pay his fares and give him a gift for helping. A few days later, he arrived, and helped us unpack our stuff, put up beds and generally make us feel so happy to be giving him something to do as well as getting to know him better. Then he told us his story.

Six months before we met, he had arrived in Greece having escaped Syria via Turkey. He had taken that ghastly boat journey, the one where smugglers force you onto flimsy rubber dinghies with an inadequate motor, and something that should hold 12 people would be rammed full with maybe 50 children, men and women each holding a bag with their possessions. Life jackets had been given them — but some hadn't even been proper ones and just had cardboard inside, not a buoyancy aid. If you objected the smugglers would pull out guns and give you a choice, take your chance or die on the beach.

Karam had made a couple of escape attempts on dinghies; some had begun to sink and they had had to return to Turkey, but on his third time of trying, he managed to get to the Greek island Chios. He nearly didn't make it as the boat took on a lot of water, as it was so overcrowded. People were crying for fear of being drowned and the men got out of the boat and hung onto the sides to try and lighten the load while others like Karam were emptying the boat of water using their shoes as makeshift buckets. It had been terrifying and dark. For years after he would have a fear of water – hardly surprising. After several hours they had finally landed on Chios and moved onto the next part of their disrupted lives.

When he did arrive, there was no welcoming committee for the boat. In 2014 refugees were often sworn at by the local police and, if coastguards caught them at sea, they would sometimes tow them back into international waters. In the early days, refugees would arrive, walk miles to the ferry port of the island they had landed on, travel to Piraeus in Athens and then figure out how they would get to mainland Europe from there. The cost to be smuggled was on average €1,200 from Turkey to Greece and over €5,000 per person to a western European country, Germany being the most popular.

Karam had arrived to stay with an uncle who had lived in Athens for the previous ten years. His uncle had married his mother's sister and they were expecting a baby.

Unfortunately, Karam had been deceived by his uncle. He had taken the money his family had sent to him for an onward journey to Germany and used it to fly to Sweden himself, leaving his pregnant wife under Karam's care.

Karam was stranded, but felt a family obligation to remain with the family relative, and a few months later a baby girl had been born. The uncle had left them no money so they had had to sell furniture for food and nappies. I began visiting them in their sparse flat where they lived in just one room.

Our friends in Athens helped Karam with part-time work. He proved to be reliable, charming, a great musician and handsome to boot! A group of young refugee guys bonded together and we tried to help them all.

Over the months we got to know Karam well. His aunt was being accommodated in a women's refuge while he began to help our friends in Athens with the growing refugee work. He had also found a faith in Jesus for himself after many months of bible study, debate, questions and discussions. Karam would often come and spend weekends with us in Chalkida and a great friendship formed.

In April 2015 we were due a visit from some friends from the UK, among them a fabulous young woman, Liz, who was a talented musician and singer. She and I had connected while I was in Frontline Church in Liverpool. Liz was like a ray of sunshine, we laughed, hung out, worshipped, sang songs and looked at writing some songs together. Then, on the first weekend met Karam and his friend Michel.

Over the next couple of weeks, we had a few events with the refugee ministry in Athens which meant we saw Karam, Michel and others a fair bit. Towards the end of the visit I thought to myself there could be a romantic relationship beginning between Liz and Karam!

Months went past before Liz was able to return in the summer. She was welcome, but I was wondering why she wanted to return so soon. Waiting for her at the airport my phone suddenly rang — just as Liz was coming into the Arrivals hall. It was Karam.

'Hello Momma.' (This was the title he had now given me!) 'It's me. I'm wondering if Liz has arrived yet.'

Liz walked up to me just at that moment! We hugged and I said: 'Someone wants to say hello!' At this point she did a little embarrassed giggle, went red and spoke to him on the phone.

'Well', I said, 'Someone's excited to have you back and obviously wants to see you soon!'

Sure enough, over the next ten days we watched as they were obviously getting closer to each other. It was a beautiful summer and the beaches were full with people enjoying their holiday time, warm sea, and long summer nights, 'Chill Box' frozen yogurt, cool wine and sundowners – it was a romantic location for anyone!

On her final day I drove Liz back to the airport and Karam was coming out by metro from Athens to say his goodbyes. Not wanting to play gooseberry, I left them for a while before Liz had to go through to security.

They parted and I put my arm around Karam and we left the departure lounge. He was silent. We walked to the car with Karam's head firmly down, looking at the ground, and I asked if he was OK. Suddenly a dam broke. He sobbed. His crying was deep and heaving. I waited and finally he spoke just three words 'I love her.'

'Does she know that?' I asked

'I didn't want to tell her, in case she doesn't feel the same way about me,' he replied

'Well, I think you should tell her because I'm pretty sure she feels the same too!'

Suddenly all the angst of the past few years and the pent-up feelings of despair, rejection and holding it together poured out; from that moment a beautiful healing process began in Karam's life.

Karam did tell her and they began a long-distance relationship that had many ups and downs over the next few years. Liz frequently came out to see him and often stayed with us. Karam took Maria and myself to buy an engagement ring and proposed to Liz on Boxing Day on the beach where they had both been baptised a few months previously!

The romance wasn't appreciated by everyone as it raised some cultural concerns but we could see two young single people who were in love and that's a powerful force to try and stop! LOVE WINS. Maybe one day you will read the full story as his journey is a book in itself but after four long years of living in Greece, Karam got permission to live in the UK, and got on a plane with his fiancée, to start a new life in England having secured a visa to enter the UK to marry. (This had involved us writing volumes of sponsoring supporting documents which Liz needed.) The process to enter the UK as a refugee legally is extremely hard and expensive and for someone like Karam almost unheard of. He was finding there were no protocols or guidelines for his situation and he often seemed to be 'the first case', but the fact that he came via another European country and had a Greek refugee passport was a helpful step. They were being supported by many prayerful people who were watching, praying and cheering them on.

Today they have been married six years and have a gorgeous young daughter. His family made it out safely from Syria and only recently, for the first time in seven years, he was reunited with them in Germany. We remain close friends and we look forward to the day when we can meet his whole family in person having heard so much from them over the years via Skype. If this had been my son, I would have been desperate for someone to look after him the way we and others did in Greece. A short while ago when looking for another photo I came across one of Karam on the night he had been in my apartment in those early days in December and sure enough It is a group photo of men chatting in a circle with Karam's face leaning out towards the camera.

RITSONA REFUGEE CAMP

In 2016, we heard about coaches full of Syrian and Afghan refugees being dropped off at an old disused camp just twenty kilometres from Chalkida. The Greek air-force had bulldozed some woodland, and set up tents that could take five people each but the land was without electricity or shower blocks, and had only 'portaloos' provided. The Greek government were setting up camps throughout the country to house the thousands of homeless refugees and Ritsona had been allocated as one of these new camps. We found it after driving around for ages and discovered a scene of chaos. No one was really in charge. A local political group were trying to help co-ordinate between the air-force, the ministry of migration and the refugees. Bottled water and food which was worse than airline food was being brought to them three times a day. There was very little for a Middle Eastern palate let alone a differing religious one to eat. Within a week there were approximately 900 refugees on this camp. Some families refused to get off the bus and chose to return to Athens when they saw the situation there. You couldn't blame them but their only other option at that point was to sleep rough on the streets in tents.

To understand what had had caused this perfect storm you need to look and understand its context. By 2016, Greece was in the grip of a very public financial crisis. The new left-wing Government had promised to talk tough in negotiations with the

EU regarding the unbearable debt Greece owed, particularly to Germany and France via various financial systems. At one point the Greeks voted overwhelmingly to reject the EU financial deal and leave the EU. The EU ignored this and banks simply switched off their guarantees of loans. For six weeks one summer, Greek people couldn't even access their own accounts as they wished. Restrictions were placed on how much cash you could withdraw each day (40 euros maximum) and the signs of panic and queues outside banks was hard to witness and comprehend.

Added to this problem was the hundreds of thousands of refugees pouring out of Syria, Northern Iraq and Afghanistan. The borders had been opened and the 'invitation' from Angela Merkel, the German chancellor, to welcome them had created a stampede of humanity escaping oppressive regimes and a chance for some to start a new life. Suddenly Greece was hit by overwhelming numbers. Amid EU disagreements about quotas and financial assistance, the EU route was quickly shut. Borders closed and thousands of refugees were trapped in Greece. This was not a good time to have this crisis land on Greece's doorstep. Now they had to build camps, creating fear and opposition from locals. As a result, they did the minimum required to assist the thousands of refugees.

A week or so after the first arrivals at Ritsona some portable showers came – three to be precise. Two were for women and one for men. An old warehouse was opened up for people to receive packages of food and sort out the clothes and shoes which kind-hearted people had donated in black plastic bags to help.

The Red Cross turned up to offer support but were only able to give out paracetamol. The refugees were told that, if they needed further medical assistance, they would have to call an ambulance themselves. That meant speaking Greek on the phone, something I still struggle to do myself. It was dire.

We were still young as a community but this crisis made Malc and I set up a charity called Elpitha Hope UK so that the donations we desperately needed could be processed and accounted for correctly. We had a wonderful bunch of trustees supporting us. We actually had a struggle to open a charity bank account, because we were a Christian-based group and we had many extra points of concern to prove including our statement of faith. We had more than our share of interesting phone calls from the Bank ethics department.

As they were deliberating, we were busy buying basics, as families at the camp struggled with sleeping on blankets and having no cooking facilities. Some pregnant women and elderly people desperately needed the blow-up mattresses we were sourcing. We bought hotplates, cutlery, cups, plates, and phone-chargers. There were few electricity points around the camp. Added to this the refugees found themselves sharing the camp space with snakes, scorpions, rats and anything else that lived in the surrounding woods.

Even though it was so basic, there was an amazing peace at the camp. Everyone you visited wanted you to sit with them and have a drink and chat. We spent hours there listening to desperate stories of escape and the dangers of travelling by sea from Turkey to Greece.

Slowly the camp became more organised. The tents were exchanged for isoboxes (portacabins) and different NGO groups came to help with children, education, and playtime; eventually a laundry opened too.

We took teams onto the camp with permission to play games with the kids, and football with the young men. We would also sit in their homes, just listening and learning and being friends. As a musician, I lost count of the number of concerts we gave, especially at Christmas. Interestingly enough, in Syria it was a recognised and celebrated event.

We met so many people, all of whom had incredible stories of escape and survival. A few families and individuals stand out from the three years we worked in the camp.

One family came rushing out of their tent towards us in May 2016. Their baby son had been born a week earlier and here he was back on the camp in extremely hot weather with flies everywhere. His body was limp, his lips discoloured and bluish, and his breathing laboured. I was with Karam who happened to be visiting us that weekend. In Arabic the father pleaded for us to do something. I felt truly helpless but turned to Karam and told him to ask the dad if I could pray for this baby.

He nodded, so I took this little one into my arms and prayed. I spoke of life and health, healing to flow into his body right away. The parents were thankful we had stopped to listen to them.

They invited us in for tea. We accepted and found four other young boys who were already part of their family. They had fled Aleppo with their house no longer in existence from the regime's bombing of the city.

We chatted about what help he could get today; they knew a local Greek couple who they called and, for a few days they left the camp to stay in their home until baby Ahmed was well enough to return to his tent. Ahmed made a full recovery. This started our connection with this family, which to this day we maintain via Facebook. One day, a photographer came onto the camp and took a photo of this mum and baby. She turned it into a life-sized oil painting and it got chosen for a prize in the BP section of the National Gallery in London. I know this because my son-in-law called me to say he had been attending a corporate event at the gallery, and had walked into the section and immediately recognised the mother and baby Ahmed. Then it became newsworthy and we watched a programme on the BBC about them and their journey and subsequent resettlement in Ireland.

Another young man we met was only six months from completing his medical training in Syria when the hospital he worked in was targeted by the regime because they were treating rebels. The officers of the army would walk into operating theatres with no sterile clothing on and give surgeons orders about who they could or could not operate on. Muhammad was assisting once when the soldiers commanded him to stop the surgery. The surgeon told them he was in charge of the Operating Room and ignored them. Suddenly there was a fight; the surgeon was assaulted and taken away and imprisoned for seven days. He was beaten and made to realise he couldn't speak to the army like that. Muhammad knew he couldn't stay. He escaped and arrived in Ritsona where we befriended him. He became the unofficial medic on site, as well as my trusted ticket seller for the buses we provided for the camp, to enable residents to travel into town twice a week for access to shops, cash machines, health needs and the beach!

Malc volunteered to teach English at the camp via another NGO. His TEFL qualification came into so much good use there.

Eventually we were invited onto the camp co-ordinating committee. We had a brilliant time linking up with all sorts of charities and government departments for over 18 months helping to provide resources for families, create a newly formed nursery and teach English. Then, after a new government came into power in the autumn of 2019 a shift began to happen. Slowly the NGOs were not having their permissions to work on the camp renewed and we began to feel that our time of being able to help could be coming to an end. After three and a half years of being welcomed onto the camp I received a WhatsApp message. It simply said that, until further notice, we would not be allowed access but that we'd need to fill in new forms and documents to carry on. Initially we began the application, but the forms and questionnaires got too onerous, and when we heard there were plans to expand the camp to accommodate 3,000 refugees we had to step back. Most of the families we had been supporting had left and, in February 2020, we kept our promise of taking a lovely Syrian family we had befriended two years earlier to the airport to begin their new life in Holland. They were being reunited with the father who had been smuggled out a year earlier.

We shared meals and life stories with these people. So many of them valued family structures and we would bring ours onto the camp to meet them, or bring them into our home. We had stumbled into refugee work, and were not trained to speak Arabic or Farsi. We often felt inadequate, but when we were asked why we did what we did, we spoke gently and sincerely about our faith.

They attended our community, stayed for our lunches and heard about the God of love that gave us the compulsion to love the person in front of us and in some small way make a difference. One of our prayers that to this day has not yet been realised was that we would have a worker dedicated to the camp from our own community. There is still such a great need, but the sacrifice is great and the wrong person could do more harm than good; sadly we have seen that happen.

BABY ABDUL

Refugee work for us came in waves. First there was the work in Athens, then in Ritsona, our local refugee camp. Then, in Feb 2019, we were contacted by a local team from the ministry of migration who asked if we would consider helping out a group of young people who had recently been housed in a disused hotel 15 kilometres away from Chalkida.

We agreed that the social worker would bring a minibus to us with students, as we now had a hub where we met as a community running youth work, workshops, and English classes. It was also where our community gathered for fellowship. This had been our dream, to have a multipurpose venue to use for the city, so when it came to renovating this basement, we did so, deliberately making it look as un-churchy as possible. It ended up with more of a lounge feel.

This first meeting with these students was just pure joy. Twelve young Afghan, Iranian and Ethiopian adults huddled into our hub enjoying the refreshments we had provided and generally chatting away to Malc who was assessing their ability so we could begin English lessons for them. As we had experienced previously in other projects, the lady who brought them suggested there could be some finance to cover some costs but was upfront in letting us know if these guys wanted to come to lessons, they would have to do so by bus or by walking as there was no funding to transport them back and forth. They agreed to come to us, but we only had an estate car so couldn't help too much. The cost of the lessons, all materials, heating, opening the hub and food would be borne by our charity Elpitha Hope UK. The finance from the government agency unsurprisingly never materialised! Giving them tasty snacks was a welcome kindness to them as the food provided at the hotel was abysmal. Most of the refugees we met were from Muslim countries and therefore had Islam as their religion. Some were very nominal, but a fair few were culturally adhering to the dress code and food requirements; amongst the group we had two women from Somalia who were deeply religious.

After a few weeks Malc noticed a young man hadn't turned up for the lesson after having been a regular attendee. So asked if anyone knew where Ali was.

'Ah, he's in hospital... here in Chalkida' came the reply.

'Is he not well?' Asked Malc.

'No, his wife has had a baby.'

It was so comical. We hadn't even known that this young man was married, let alone that he was about to become a father. After the lesson Malc and I decided to visit him and his wife, knowing full well that Greek hospitals didn't offer much in terms of attending to your needs like they do in the UK. Your family are expected to help wash you, bring food, attend to your needs and, as a young refugee couple, this would not be happening for them.

When we arrived, we found his wife tearfully sitting on her bed, with Ali beside her looking helpless. We greeted them then simply asked where the baby was.

'He's not here, and I don't know where he is!' cried Ali's wife, Shazia.

They'd had a baby boy the day before and had been told there was something wrong with their baby and he would need to go to a baby's hospital in Athens.

Twenty-four hours on and they knew no more. They didn't know where he was or how he was. Even worse, no one in the hospital seemed concerned about finding out.

I could feel my emotions rise: a mix of indignation and anger. I simply asked for the social worker's phone number based back at the hotel and began a conversation with a woman who was clearly indifferent to this young couple's plight.

I spoke firmly and calmly, letting her know we were friends of this couple and perhaps she could find out where the baby was, and how he was and I asked her to make sure his mother was reunited with him as soon as possible.

I knew Shazia had been in touch with Christian aid workers on an island when they first arrived in Greece (someone had called me that day from Athens to tell me this!) and, as I understood she was open to hearing about our faith, I asked if we could pray together that Jesus would look after her baby and we would find him so she could be re-united.

She nodded enthusiastically and, through her tears, smiled and thanked me. Another night passed before we had a reply; she called back to say she had been told which Athens hospital the baby was in, that he was doing OK, and that the parents should go back to the hotel; the baby would be back with them in a few days. That simply wasn't an option for these young parents, and we totally agreed with their decision. A few hours later, with our help, Shazia checked out of Chalkida hospital. She'd had a caesarean birth and hadn't been washed or even properly fed. More importantly she wanted to breast feed her baby, and time was running short to get her milk flowing for her to have that option. We took them back to our flat, where they showered, washed, ate and rested for a few hours. I gave her some of my clothes and then we headed to Athens to find baby! We bought a breast pump en route, so, on the way into Athens by car, she and Ali began to express milk for her baby. That was a definite first for us!

We finally found the hospital and, after speaking to a few staff tracked their baby down to the 5th floor ward.

We rang the bell; out came a nurse who did speak English. Astonishingly she told them they would have to wait until visiting hours. It was at this point that I just said 'NO!' I'd had enough. It hurts so much when you feel people are not being treated with dignity. I know how it feels to live in a foreign land without full command of their language or culture, but there has to be a basic humanitarian decency in our responses, surely?

'No, my friend' I said 'This is the mother and she needs to be with her baby now, not later, we can all wait outside but not his mother. She wants to feed him, hold him and, after 48 hours, it's vital this happens now!'

Probably a bit surprised that this English woman was pushing back, she reluctantly agreed Shazia could go in and see him. After 30 minutes, I was allowed in too. Baby was being drip fed via his scalp and he was linked up to a few machines, which made it all look more serious than it actually was.

Fortunately, we found a wonderful doctor who explained they had received this baby 48 hours ago via ambulance with no notes or explanation and presumed he might have diabetes and so were trying to sort out his feeding issues. As it turned out, the baby was fine and, after this crazy day, they allowed the parents to stay with the baby. They said that, as long as Shazia could feed him, they would let him go within a couple of days. Mum and baby were happily reunited! They also decided to give him a western name after an aid worker they'd first met on the island of Lesvos. We laughed at the thought he could have been called Malcolm!

The young couple became friends and, for six months, they came to our community for English lessons and some of our meetings. They heard very clearly about the love God has for them and the transforming power of a relationship with Jesus. We have on-going discussions now about faith and, even when they were relocated to a new hotel one and a half hours' drive away from us, we still visited to catch up when we could. Three years on they have now legally moved from Greece to Germany.

DARK HOURS AND TESTING TIMES

In late 2019 we attended a Christian conference titled 'Go Viral'. It was a brilliant event packed with amazing speakers and encounters with God. One prophetic moment happened while listening to a female speaker, Danielle Strickland; she had only just made it to the conference due to difficulties with the flight out of the US, but she brought a word that so resonated with me I was crying throughout the whole talk. It was about when disruption comes: not if, but when. She talked about the different stages of change and transition and our responses to it.

I wasn't interested in the coffee break afterwards, just in prayer to seal into my spirit what I had heard and then some time out to mull over what God was saying.

We welcomed 2020 in and before we could get our breath the disruption started. A hand operation for Malc required him to stay in the UK while I returned to Greece to restart the new term and focus in on more prayer. There were a few weeks of God's presence showing up heavily in the community and upon us; then my mum had a serious illness, which required me to return early, just after Malc had returned to Greece.

After a wonderful tank-filling prayer conference in Liverpool with our home church where Peter Greig, leader of the 24/7 Prayer Movement had been speaking, we headed to Spain to pastorally visit two overseas families. It was a significant time of ministry.

On our return to Greece in early March, we found a wave of panic hitting Europe over a virus that had originated from China and was quickly spreading worldwide where people were dying in huge numbers. Greece went into a very hard and early lockdown, leaving us with the choice of where to be confined. Since we were already having our meetings remotely on-line as we could no longer gather in groups, we reasoned it would be best to return to the UK in case our family needed us so we flew back. We had no idea at this point that we would be unable to see our kids and grandchildren. We flew back into the UK on my birthday, seeing mainly empty airports and planes on the way.

Bang. The heavy gate shut, and what we had thought would only be a month or so turned into 16 weeks of staying local and cancelling all our travel plans and holidays. We had disruption to a high degree.

We watched the regular TV updates almost in shock and wept with grieving families. We prayed fervently for all those in positions of authority as it was clear the government were in a tail-spin. And who wouldn't be?

2020 was meant to be the busiest year for our friends and family to visit us in Greece but everything just kept being cancelled. When the summer arrived, to take a flight you not only had the usual security measures but now you were having to take Covid tests, fill in passenger locator forms which would give data protection a run for its money, and wear masks. By the autumn we were also quarantining and spending inordinate times of isolation, which have had a deep and profound effect.

This is how I came to write down these stories. I suddenly had days upon days of spare time. We were rarely going out except for a daily walk, and having the new strange experience of food shopping with queues, social distancing and the generally unpleasant feeling of a familiar life being taken over by a threat. It reminded me of the time flying changed forever after 9/11. We did not know how long these new practices would have to stay in place.

Overall, came a feeling of displacement. We were no longer in our normal environment. This disrupted life meant we had to find new rhythms of grace, devotion and separation from our God family in Greece and Liverpool. We spent many hours on Zoom and other social media platforms connecting with friends, church leaders, trustees and even our own kids!

TESTING TIMES

In the summer of 2020, we had just made it back to Greece after being away for 16 long weeks, after numerous previous flights had been cancelled due to countries drawing up contingency plans with only passengers from 'safe nations' being allowed to travel. When we finally made it back, the UK was on most countries' 'naughty list' due to unbelievably high numbers of deaths. It had become a costly commitment to return, for which our friends and supporters of the work helped cover the cost. It took us two days to arrive, travelling via Amsterdam and being tested on arrival. I was given the all-clear and we began to settle back into our Greek routine and life.

When we unravelled our summer carpet, having rolled up the winter ones, the lounge carpet disintegrated; something had been spilt on it, leaving a large threadbare patch and making us wonder what could have caused it. It was man-made fibre so not moths!

After three days we were heading out mid-afternoon for our first swim of the year. We decided to check out our favourite beach, so took our car. Our smaller new apartment that we had moved to two years earlier after the amazing large apartment by the sea was in a small square filled with trees. It was very close to town and where our community hub was, and not far from the sea. But the roads were busy and this afternoon it was taking a few minutes for the traffic to calm. Finally, a lady slowed her car down to let us out, and all the other vehicles behind her also stopped. Unfortunately a motorcyclist decided to overtake all these cars and realised far too late we were pulling out. He crashed into the driver's side of the car. The thump was sickening, and so loud. The young man rolled onto our bonnet. These things happen so quickly you go into emergency mode. My nursing training came to the fore and the first thought I had was for his safety. Remarkably, he was only badly bruised on one leg and, thankfully, he had been wearing a helmet, which is quite unusual in Greece!

Within minutes, the car was pulled over to the side of the road; spectators had withdrawn from their shop doors and balconies, and we were discussing the damage to our car and his bike when we realised the young man did not want to be caught having had an accident. He was driving his dad's bike, which was insured but he himself had no licence to drive. He pleaded with us to settle privately. We did consider this but after quickly phoning some of our community they told us if our vehicle was badly damaged, the insurance company would not pay out if we chose not to involve the police. This actually was our third 'no-fault' accident in seven years; the process of informing companies, police, paperwork takes hours and is all the more stressful when you can't speak the language fluently. Sadly, when the police came out to the accident, the officer told us it was the third time this young man had been found without a licence. Each time, he had promised them he would go and take the driving test. He hadn't and here we were with a very badly damaged car.

Photos were taken, paperwork was completed and everyone disappeared. In this situation, they probably go home to their families, chat about the incident, maybe someone makes them a cuppa, and gives them a hug. We send a WhatsApp message to our kids, tell them we're OK, get a sympathetic response and that's it. AND THAT'S IT! Unkind, horrible events have come our way; we constantly get pushed back emotionally by things. My wonderful dad had died of cancer when I was in South Africa, and despite coming back to help Mum and see him several times in the first nine months of our relocating, the cancer was aggressive and quick; it took him before I could return to hold his hand and say my final goodbye.

Our kids have faced illness and trauma; we've had attempted break-ins and been defrauded out of money; life at times has been very dark. You don't deny these moments, they are indeed valley experiences but we never lost hope, nor our unswerving belief that God knows and cares.

In November 2020, we experienced lockdown Greek style. This lockdown prohibited you from leaving your home unless you sent an SMS message from your phone with different codes for leaving. Code 1 was to see a doctor. Code 2 was for shopping right up to Code 6 for exercise. We saw police stopping our neighbours and checking their permission texts. Malc got stopped and spot-checked; if you didn't have the correct permission and ID card you were fined €300. It felt so draconian. By mid-December, with no release or un-locking of restrictions in sight we had to make a decision as to where we were going to be for Christmas. My mum had become terminally ill, so we decided to leave Greece and return to the UK.

We arrived just as the prime minister changed the plans for Christmas gatherings and unfortunately this meant we couldn't see our kids or grandchildren. Back we went into another 16-week lockdown, which seemed even harder. It was much more of a struggle to stay positive.

Then there was us! We were together in a way that would probably test any long-term relationship. After decades of marriage which judged by its best parts were loving and devoted, we were facing up to some habits that had taken hold, with some behaviours that were not glorifying to God nor loving towards each other.

We had a choice: bury it, and look the other way, or call it, own it and get help! We chose the latter and received counselling, personal prayer and ministry.

We have always wanted to be the best partner for each other and, though at times we have failed in this, for the most part we have succeeded so we won't beat ourselves up constantly but dust ourselves down and remember all the biblical heroes who also tripped up in their pursuit of His Kingdom.

Sadly, some relationships in our Greek community were put under too much lockdown strain; some simply could not cope with Zoom meetings and our absence. It became incredibly challenging maintaining unity from so far away without real personal contact and with bilingual communication.

We stayed in good connection with our wonderful friends in Greece, but the length of time away had become a defining time for us, which we felt was God-ordained. By the time we returned in spring 2021, we began talks to transition out of the Greek work, sensing it was time to release the local ministry to a small leadership team. Transitioning isn't easy, the 'not knowing', 'what next?' and uncertainty can be very unsettling. However, we have always taken one step at a time and continued to look to God for His leading in our lives.

UNFINISHED SYMPHONY

In the summer of 2021 we had a 'suddenly' moment of God. We had begun the process of transitioning out from Greece, and the community hub, which we'd used for five years was having to close. It was made slightly easier by the landlords asking us to sign a new two-year rental increasing the rental amount; this seemed ridiculous as we had rarely used it through nearly 18 months of lockdown. Then a passing casual remark from my mum when I was back in the UK let me know that a local church of England in Bath was advertising a senior associate minister's post for the second time having failed to appoint the first time. I wasn't sure if this would be of interest to Malc, but I passed it on and, to my surprise, he seemed keen to pursue it. Within weeks he had applied, and by the August he had been successful in his interview and offered the post.

We were stunned when he got the call back, delighted for this new door of opportunity but saddened to think it meant our Greek adventure was definitely drawing to a close. We returned in the autumn of 2021 to begin to hand over the work and Malc started his new post in Bath part-time. My mum had been battling a liver cancer during the previous 18 months and her attendance at Malc's induction was almost the last time she was seen in public by many of her church friends. She passed away late in October with me by her side, holding her hand and gently singing to her. I didn't feel sadness immediately, just relief she was free from the pain she had been bearing so well. However the loss of a mother hurts, no matter how old you are; I felt the pain over time, and still do. Not owning our own home Malc's appointment meant for the next few years we have somewhere to live which we are truly grateful for.

Another shock came to us early 2022 when my younger brother Jon passed away suddenly aged 61. Just months after my mum's death, we were plunged once again into mourning and a funeral. 'Life is fragile, handle with care'; I read that on a poster, and it seems very true.

My greatest joy has to be that, in the last few years, I've become a grandparent. The Greeks call their grandmas 'Yia Yia' and it's a very easy thing for my little ones to call me. So, it's back to baby cuddles, toddler mess and early learning fun.

Over the years if we have experienced difficult financial times, we have also experienced times of abundance and on occasion have given away cars, money and even a house at a lower than market value price, all because we have felt God was telling us to do so.

Years ago, I heard a saying that 'You can't out-give God' – I have already mentioned this earlier, and it's so true. Sometimes He waits to see if we have grown too comfortable or safe in our lack of trust in Him. However, ultimately, He is the perfect parent and has been with us through every high and every low. And we know He will stay with us until we breathe our last or He returns!

Higher Heights, Deeper Seas

'THERE ARE HIGHER HEIGHTS'

Chorus
There are higher heights for me
There are deeper seas where I want to be,
Reaching out and breaking boundaries
Call to the wild, speak to this child
Awaken me

Verse 1
Though I walk through the valley
I will fear no ill
Your presence right beside me
Telling me be still.

Bridge
You're my inspiration
You're my guiding light
Lead me out of darkness
To hear the songs of Life

Verse 2
Take away the fear that's stopping
This heart from being brave
I'm stepping out to new horizons

Higher Heights, Deeper Seas

And asking you for faith.

Fill me with a passion,
Show me the mountain climb
The mighty God of all creation
Can be a friend of mine!

Trish Morgan
© Radical UK Music 2022

Contact Details

If you would like to invite Trish to speak at an event please contact her via the following email:

greatadventuresig@gmail.com

Or you can follow her on Facebook

Trish Morgan - Singer/Songwriter

Her songs can be found on Spotify, Youtube and Apple iTunes

To see photographs outlining the stories in this book please open the QR code.

Printed in Great Britain
by Amazon